"You Are God"

The Enlightened Luciferian

Written By:

Simon Mark Alvarez

YOU

ARE

GOD

-*Introduction*-

Unless, you are a Luciferian, or interested in Luciferiniasm, or perhaps you're just not or no longer religious, or you question a lot of things that most people will not question because of fear and resentment leaned towards them, or if you are at the bare minimum, open minded, this book is for you. It describes in detail the basics of Luciferianism, although, there is additional information that I had intended to place in this book; but I will save for its sequel; as I intend to write a trilogy for this novel. Because, of some sexuality that I mention in this book, I advise strongly that reading discretion is highly advised for those underage. Some (actually many) will not like this book because I constantly attack religion left and right; but I do it because I believe in the preservation of the human species and I truly believe that religion is the greatest obstacle to this; as nearly every war on earth (from history to currently) has been fought over which religion is accurate; resulting in millions and millions of lives exterminated. Yet, its survivors of mankind (us) are left clueless of which is the right religion? This is one basic question; and if you are a Luciferian, my attacks on religion will indeed enlighten you; and probably put a nice little smile on your face. For those of you who are offended at this or will be offended, as a Luciferian, I am not here to judge you or say that you're the ignorant one. As a Luciferian, I must respect (although disagree) with your opinion and judgments based on the topics that I discuss here in my book. If there is some information missing in here in regards to the ideas of Luciferiniasm, I will not forget to mention it in the Enlightened Luciferian II! This

4

book is meant to demonstrate, encourage, & supply the reader with enlightened energy & knowledge. In no way, is it meant to be a book upholding any religion. On the contrary, it is designed to encourage every human being on planet earth to ignore their personal religion, to burn their bibles or sacred religious artifacts, and answer only to themselves and not their divine entity (God) in the hopes by a stroke of luck to receive what it is that they (the people) have prayed for. This book is a proclamation of establishing the fact that we are all God's. I will say that again! *"You are a God!"* The illusion that something or somebody is more powerful than you, is the illusion that religion wants you to believe. You control your fate & destiny! You control your own life! Best of all, you control your own world! If you notice, throughout this book, I repeat a lot of the same and/or relevant information because I want to keep constantly reminding you of the necessary information that you need to program your mind with the mentality of *"You can accomplish and conquer any obstacle in your life that threatens your attempt to reach success!"* My aim is to make sure that you are the target; I am the one with the rifle; and instead of shooting a bullet, I am aiming to shoot wisdom and knowledge at you. You are my target; and my only desire in this book is to make sure that you use the wisdom available in this novel to get whatever it is that you want, whenever you want. Many of you will read a few pages of this book; and put it down; either because you do not have any personal time to yourself or because I make no sense. I must (and will), as an author of this debatable book, respect and honor your personal conclusion and judgment. After all, me and you, are *"God's"* and this is our world; and I am the symbol of the Serpent, not here to deceive you, but to enlighten you...

5

I

"I am who I am!" –Yahweh (God) Exodus 3:14

Do you ever or did you ever wonder, (whether you are religious or not) what that special meaning, of what God told Moses in the Book of Genesis, in the Old Testament, "I am what I am" symbolizes and/or represents? I will you tell you exactly what it represents. It represents (in a hidden secret code in the bible) exactly what or who you are (the reader)! What brought you to the "New Age" section at your local bookstore (or online) to search or seek for relevant topics on the doctrine (law) of attraction; or your interest in theories about the world that you know exist or at least want to believe & feel that it exists yet is not officially recognized or acknowledged by any scientific evidence and/or government? You are a person who is open-minded; and what an enormous and special gift that you were born with! You are also a person who is willing to observe 'specific' wisdom at your own pace and/or limits; and based upon that wisdom that you are enduring, you inevitably also choose just how much wisdom you are willing to allow yourself to embrace. Everyone who has a conscious mind; and is able to do the basic necessities in order to survive (work, buy groceries, paying off a mortgage, establishing credit etc.) are capable of doing, experiencing, & receiving whatever it is that that person desires; there are no limitations to what you want in your

6

lifetime. At the end of the day, typically after a long hard (or easy) day of work, when we come home, we more than often, fantasize about never having to return back to work and instead, we fantasize about being wealthy, having our bills paid forever, being able to travel the world without any obstacles or limits (or any other applicable problems). Then, the next day when we go to work, we hope that somehow or something will change for the better for ourselves. We will get a raise, we will get promoted, even the possibility of being transferred to a more closer, and convenient location that is more preferable to us (closer to home yay!). We hope for something to change for us; but it never happens! That is because of one-single-fact... We somehow (whether we admit or not) have lost confidence in ourselves to prosper and elevate ourselves towards prosperity. The fact that we wanted that raise and promotion (as an example), but without a burning desire, that raise or promotion was never established. The fact that when we had a burning desire to get a raise and a promotion, we wanted it so bad, obsessing about it, all day and every day, but that simple (yet ever most powerful) feeling of doubt was the main obstacle to never receiving our burning desires. Doubt and lack-of-confidence, is mankind's worst enemy. I will say it again. Doubt and lack-of confidence is mankind's worst enemy! Not even the most disciplined and greatest soldier (or other military personnel) who is currently engaged or previously engaged in combat against the enemy, has a greater enemy than himself. Think about it; while the chances of survival in combat depends upon a roll-of-the-dice (chance); a soldier who is self-disciplined and has confidence enough in himself to assist his fellow-soldiers in battle; greatly increases the chances of eliminating his opposing forces

7

with his fellow-soldiers. Somehow, and yet so strangely that confidence is a key-ingredient of saving lives in battle (and also in the civilian life). The soldier that lacks confidence & self-discipline is a greater threat to himself and his fellow-soldiers while in combat. Not knowing how or what to do sometimes in life is natural; but in battle, every reaction that is demonstrated on the battlefield is crucial in determining survival and history for each opposing forces. That soldier, while he may have someone on the opposing forces trying to kill him by any means necessary, surely mankind can never have a greater enemy than himself. His or her confidence is the sword and the shield that conquers any fear and/or doubt that that person is always in danger of feeling; that most terrible and dreadful, so horrible word that should be removed from every-single dictionary and every human-beings mentality; that deprives humanity of success and prosperity, "doubt!" Confidence, on the other hand, (faith in yourself and not a higher being) greatly increases the chances of successfully receiving whatever it is that that person (or you) most desperately want(s). So exactly what is it that you truly want in your life? Do you want a brand new house, car, romance with a new partner or the desire to seek a new partner? Do you want the ability to travel without the constant worry of having sufficient funds in your bank-account? What is it that you truly want? The greatest inventors and discoverers (Benjamin Franklin & Henry Ford) in the history of our world will tell you the same thing that I am only here to remind you of; what these men have previously revealed in the past, that our destiny and future is determined based upon our feelings and desires; as well as our emotions. Unfortunately, as well, "what we don't want in are our lives." I imagine that most people do not ever get what they

8

want and/or desire because of the constant feeling of choosing something that you don't want rather than what you do want; regardless of either desire, both are very powerful. Think of what you don't want as your worst enemy; a snake that is hidden yet ready to strike you from the corner of any tree or bush as you run past it during your jog or hike. Who the hell in the world wants to get bitten by a snake? Who wants to worry about the possibility of poison slowly (or quickly) seeping through your veins and slowly injuring and/or killing you from the inside? Perhaps, I am exaggerating; but at the end of the day, whatever we constantly think about "not wanting," indeed we will endure, encounter, and/or receive everything we do not want. I will use myself as an example (true story by the way). You may have heard at least once in your lifetime (now a 2nd time again for me, but again it's my fault this happened), the phrase or quotation, "you never forget your first love." I sure as hell will never forget mine. Not because, I still have feelings for her, but because I never forgot my first (or my second) heartbreak. Her name was Stephanie. She was beautiful, smart, intelligent, articulate, creative, romantic, affectionate, and encouraged me to follow my passions and/or dreams. I was sixteen years old at the time; and although it did take time to fall-in-love with her, it didn't take too long. I fell in love with her; and did not want anybody else. I was so seriously dedicated in this relationship that I would ignore every (and) any other girl who even expressed some sort of interest in me. I wouldn't even stare at women walking past my direction. I would not acknowledge their presence. Although, I was never religious in any part of my life, I acted as if staring at other women was a sin. Of course, that wasn't the reason why I wouldn't want to stare or acknowledge other women.

9

I did not acknowledge other women out of loyalty and compassion for my future wife; as I would hope that she would become eventually. I was always faithful to every woman that I ever dated. I also expected that same thing in return. In the beginning, when I first fell in love, I was insecure (not because of low-self-esteem) but because I couldn't accept or allow anybody else to take away something so special, something so beautiful, something so perfect in every way, away from me. Not to sound conceded or anything, although being conceded isn't necessarily a bad thing, but I was very popular in my first high school (and a loner in my other three high schools). Although, I knew a lot of people in high school, there was only one girl that I ever wanted to spend the rest of my life with. I knew she was the one! Nobody could replace Stephanie. We were deeply in love. Everything seemed perfect between us. Except, there were two problems! One, I obviously knew but always ignored they're "biasness" (my parents and all of my friends hated Stephanie for their own personal reasons) and the second problem was that Stephanie ended up to be unfaithful in our relationship. Upon discovering her unfaithfulness and confronting her about it, my life shattered. I never felt the same again about any relationship. I also wanted to die. It was hard to eat, sleep, or do anything without her in the front and the back of my mind. Nothing distracted me from her. I also still ignored other women coming on to me because it wasn't the same. I took the heartbreak like a man without any distractions (and without liquor as I was underage). I asked for no help or guidance from anyone. I absorbed love no longer as something great and everlasting, but something that is hateful and evil. After getting engaged with Stephanie, and upon us going our separate ways, I never asked for the

10

engagement ring back that I bought her. I let her keep it for one reason only: so that she can never forget me. I am sure that she never will; but if she ever does, it will probably be for the best. Obviously, when our friendship, relationship, engagement, and future ended, I regretted both ever meeting her and also ever giving my heart to somebody. However, seven years later, I think the opposite now. I am glad that it happened. First of all, a heartbreak, while painful and so horrible it will inevitably be; in the end, it makes you stronger and able to endure and embrace anything relevant or much worse than a heartbreak (Its really true). You know the feeling now. But that feeling, although it was so horrible to you, made you a better & stronger person. It made you understand and appreciate love. It opened your eyes. It sure opened mine. Now, I am very, very, very, very, very, very, selective of who I want to date. But the reason I am mentioning this as an example, is because now I know that the circumstances that I experienced with Stephanie were not her fault; on the contrary, it was all my fault. No, I didn't cheat, mentally or physically abuse her in any way. I did break one promise to her: "that I would never break up with her." But, I declare without any doubt that this relationship terminated because of my mentality. My brain frequencies that I channeled and submitted to the universe (the entire world) gave me my response back. I submitted to the universe (the entire world) my brain frequencies of the most desired fear that I know for a fact comes across every human-beings mind at least a couple times in their life before, during, or after a relationship. That feeling is a "don't want" feeling. I must confess that I had two powerful and common "don't want" feelings during my relationship before it terminated. The first "don't want" feeling was "I do not want to ever

11

breakup!" The second "don't want" feeling was, "I don't want her to ever cheat on me." In the beginning when we fell in love, I had the first "don't want" feeling constantly even though our relationship was healthy. I suppose that I felt this way because I didn't want anybody else to try and take her away from my life. The second "don't want" feeling started to appear in my mind frequently after our third break-up. (We were together for almost four years and broke up on-and-off seven times within those four years). Our break-ups only lasted a few weeks at the most. They were more like separations or breaks so-to-speak. I will not say in this book how or when I discovered her unfaithfulness; but I will admit that I am convinced that this occurred because of my constant "don't want" thoughts that I submitted to the universe. The universe responded to my powerful emotions and desires of "not wanting" to break up and have an unfaithful partner. The universe did not do this because it hates me. The universe after all, gave me what I wanted from the beginning which was a relationship with someone. I didn't want something and I got it. It's not because opposites attract! It's because of my negative thoughts (don't wants) that responded to my commands or requests. I am convinced that if I thought or continued to think during the time (seven years ago) that me and Stephanie were a couple, of positive thoughts, "do wants" instead of "don't wants," that I would still be with her till this very day. Had I thought, that I wanted or desired to be happy with her, or I want to have a family with her, I want to feel our future baby kick inside her beautiful tummy, I want us to get married on a beach, I want, I want, I want, I want... Had I continued down this positive path, it would no doubt in my mind, occurred. Fate does not decide anything for anybody unless you believe it

12

does. However, faith is more powerful and stronger than fate. Faith is the main ingredient of the recipe that is required to accomplish the steps of making your dinner or beverage. Your beverage (coffee) consists of recipes and ingredients. If faith is the main (and most superior) ingredient (having faith that the coffee machine will successfully heat up the water required for your coffee) while preparing your beverage (coffee), what is the recipe? The Recipe is simple! You already acknowledge the faith that is already inside your mind (strong belief) believing that the coffee machine will operate without any issues. You are convinced that your coffee machine is not broken. As a result, there is absolutely no reason why it should not function; considering the fact that its electrical cord is plugged in into the electrical socket; and there is a bright light above you (illumination); indicating that you have paid, like always, your electric bill. Now, what is the recipe? The recipe is putting the coffee inside the cup along with some milk; perhaps maybe some coffee creamer (or sugar, for those sugar lovers). Those are very simple steps. Add everything together with hot water, and you have successfully created a cup of coffee. The doctrine of attraction is exactly the same way. You must always have un-denying faith in yourself in order to successfully create your destiny with your recipes (your desires of cars, houses, romance, love, marriage, job, travel, retirement). Remember, your desire is your recipe; (the coffee and sugar or what it is that you frequently want)! Your faith is the main ingredient to successfully make that happen (coffee machine or the universe responding to your un-denying faith!) What do you desire? Does it make you happy? Does it put a smile across that beautiful face of yours (you must always believe that you are beautiful)? If it

13

does, why not accept or believe in yourself that you can obtain and/or receive it? Depending upon your circumstances, it may not always be easy to believe this. Doubt has always been a natural feeling for every human being. Unfortunately, doubt is the #1 most evil definition and feeling that any human being can bestow upon him or herself. To be able to live a life of abundance, doubt must forever be removed from your vocabulary and mentality. Just remember, to always have a burning desire combined (mixed) with emotions of having a non-stop passion of establishing a positive outlook on whatever it is that you desire. Also, always remember, that "I want" will always overpower "I don't want!" Disregard the mentality of believing in "I don't want!" It is not your friend; it is your worst enemy; since you are inviting the universe to give in to your demands of anything that "you don't want!" As a Luciferian, you must rely and believe in yourself always; no matter the circumstances against you; your worship in another entity and/or religion will betray you, lie to you, and lead (and leave) you in directions where you will inevitably be lost; because you do not exactly know what it is that satisfies your God. As a Luciferian, you are not worshipping the devil or Satan as some people think or associate Lucifer with such an alleged evil-entity. You are worshipping yourself, convinced without any doubt that you are capable of establishing your future with your own, powerful, belief in yourself. The great thing about being a Luciferian is that you don't have to be an atheist and/or devoted Christian to become a Luciferian. You can believe in anything that you desire or want; because what brings you eternal happiness is what matters (even if your happiness is selfishness to others perception); whether it be good or bad. Lucifer, the serpent who appeared to Adam

14

desired to give Adam enlightened intelligence. After all, what good was it for Adam and Eve to be born without any intelligence? Lucifer was the fallen angel who enlightened the very first human-beings on earth; but he was not the only fallen angel as there were many who contributed to the preservation of the human species. Remember, God lied to Adam and Eve; that they would both die if they ate (yet alone touch the fruit) from the tree that is in the middle of the garden (commonly known as the tree of enlightened intelligence).

"But, from the fruit of the tree which is in the middle of the garden, you shall not eat from it or touch it, or you will die." – Genesis 3:3

The serpent (Lucifer) appeared to Eve and convinced her to eat the fruit from the tree; which she inevitably did; If it is true, did she die immediately from this alleged poisonous fruit as God promised that both her and Adam would die upon eating it? Well, before Eve debated whether or not to listen to God or Lucifer (the serpent), she was convinced that Lucifer (the serpent) coming from God, was pure & honest. Indeed, he was honest until the end!

"You will not certainly die; for God knows that when you eat from it, your eyes will be opened; and you will be like God, knowing good and evil!" – (Lucifer) Genesis 3:4

"The woman (Eve) was convinced. She saw that the tree was beautiful and its fruit looked delicious; and she wanted the wisdom (Superior Intelligence as God) it would give her. So she took some of the fruit and ate it. Then she gave some to her husband (Adam), who was with her, and he ate it, too." – Genesis 3:6

15

"Then, the eyes of both of them (Adam and Eve) were opened; and they realized that they were naked; so they sewed fig leaves together and made coverings for themselves." – Genesis 3:7

Reading the Book of Genesis is very interesting; not because of its "alleged" accurate historical-account, but because, it obviously acknowledges that God is imperfect. He has flaws. He makes mistakes. He is immortal; and he is not perfect. Because, apparently, God apparently sees everything; but did not see Lucifer deceive Adam and Eve. However, through countless times in the bible, God is acknowledging that he sees, hears, and knows everything that you do. This is the Universe by the Doctrine of Attraction; not the God that is portrayed somewhere in the clouds or in heaven. So, either God is lying to his prophets and/or messengers to spread his holy messages to the general population, and he is perfect and flawless; but allowed Lucifer to allegedly deceive Eve; or God is imperfect and flawed, and never knew that the serpent (that he cast down himself from heaven) would again, allegedly betray him by convincing Eve that eating from the fruit of the tree would not kill her. So far, Lucifer has not lied; in fact, he spoke the truth. God is the one who deceived Eve; by installing this fear into her image that the tree of good and knowledge was evil and tainted. God, if he really was powerful, could have seen all this coming; instead, he let it happen; and yet blames the serpent (Lucifer) for the wisdom and intelligence that humans have acquired through the works of Lucifer; which God did not want humans to acquire. I often wonder that since God admits and confesses that he has created everything on planet-Earth, why would he make a tree that threatens his superiority? I believe that humans and God (the Universe)

16

are equally powerful amongst each other. Neither is superior above the other. Another point that I must confess before I continue with the enlightened-story of Adam and Eve, is that when God made human-beings, he regretted it so bad. God is an emotional entity. Anything emotional (such as human-beings), is imperfect and flawed; as he demonstrates with his persistent and unsympathetic threat and determination to exterminate every species and living organism on planet earth. I understand that this world has produced the worst tyrannical human beings on earth! However, what did animals (even extinct dinosaurs) ever do to planet-Earth to deserve such massive extinction far worse than any human-being has ever conceived of doing and/or carrying out with evil actions? Why should other living species have to pay the price for one (humans) species? I will get back to this debate; now let's go back to the debate between Adam and Eve, and God.

"Then the man and his wife heard the sound of the Lord God as he was walking in the garden in the cool of the day, and they hid from the Lord God among the trees of the garden." – Genesis 3:8

Obviously, God couldn't see everything inside the Garden of Eden because he couldn't even find Adam and Eve. Either, God pretended not to know (lying again) or like humans, he is limited to the basic five senses; which is see, hear, touch, smell, and taste. This can only mean that God is not superior above humans; he is equal as us humans.

But the lord God called to the man, "Where are you?" - Genesis 3:9

Obviously, the fruit from the "tree of knowledge of good and evil" did two things to Adam and Eve. The first one, is

17

that it permanently gave Adam and Eve the basic five senses; in addition with the opportunity to understand and practice the Doctrine (law) of Attraction. Remember, God did not want any of this! God wanted to make sure that humans were inferior to him; no different than for centuries that the white man believed that he (the white race) was superior against all races. Do you notice these similarities? In Islam, according to the Quran, (allegedly true) Satan, when asked by God, (Allah) to bow before his first human creation (Adam), Satan (A Jinn) refused and commented that he was "superior to Adam because he (Satan) was made of fire, while Adam is inferior because he was made simply from clay." This sounds equivalent to the mentality of specific races who are convinced that they are superior above minority races. So, even in Heaven, the debate of superior races against minorities is a debate; not just in our modern world. I never understood why Lucifer is considered so evil and sinister; when he provided infinite wisdom and knowledge to the first humans on earth for the sake of preserving their existence. It also must be noted that Lucifer never asked Adam and Eve to worship him (Lucifer) instead of God; all he really did was encourage Eve to eat the fruit from the "tree of knowledge of good and evil." He also never lied to Adam and Eve; so really, what was his sin? After all, isn't the ninth commandment written by the "finger of God" himself stating that: "Thou shall not bear false witness?"

"Then the lord God said to the woman, what is this, you have done?" The woman said, "The serpent deceived me, and I ate." Genesis 3:13

Eve, obviously, does not take responsibility for her free-choice of eating or not eating the fruit from the "tree of

18

knowledge of good and evil." Instead, she blames Lucifer. God is convinced and believes her. But it's God's fault for placing what he cast down from heaven in the same place that his first creations of mankind were also located. Did God really believe that Lucifer would not educate his first creation of mankind and convince mankind that wisdom and intelligence is superior above submitting to an entity; that humans will never see, feel, hear, touch, or taste in their lifetime; only upon experiencing death (allegedly)? It's pretty obvious that God adores and encourages lack of knowledge and lack of evolution. After all, superior intelligence is a threat to his existence and his power. If people only knew that their mind is the most powerful weapon that gives them everything that they need, want, desire, love, and cherish. God doesn't decide what you get or don't get; you decide what you get or don't get. The only thing that you have no control of is when you will receive it to some extent. The extent is based on how bad your burning desire really is. If it is on fire, it will go slow or medium; if the burning desire is to the point of your mind melting, than it will be received faster. Lucifer never wanted to be above humans; he wanted to be above God! In reality, God, Lucifer, and humans are equal. There is no difference. There never has been. There never will be. After condemning Adam and Eve, Adam, with having to work all the days of his life, and Eve (and all women) having to go through painful child-bearing; and the serpent (Lucifer) having to crawl on his belly for eternity, God then decided to not kill either Adam and Eve by his own will or he knew that the fruit from the tree would not kill Eve all along. Instead, he installs this twisted and sinister fear of trying to convince bible-readers that nobody is responsible for their own lives. We are all paying because of one human being

19

(Eve) who took and ate from the fruit of the "tree of knowledge of good and evil." I am convinced and confess, that every human being is responsible for his or her own actions; regardless of what their mentality perceives. Apparently, and like a human, God decided to tolerate Adam and Eve; not because he is a kind and loving, and forgiving God, but because he simply changed his mind. If the book of Genesis is accurate, then God never forgave their actions and condemned all of mankind for Eve's actions. Bush's still have thorns, every living species on earth must eat or will die of starvation; and women still go through painful child-bearing. Yeah, God sure is a forgiving entity. After all, he could change or do anything that he desires; if he really can, he never saw his own enemy coming (Lucifer) but the greatest ally of mankind.

"The lord God made garments of skin for Adam and his wife and clothed them." – Genesis 3:21

Below is my most favorite biblical verse in the Book of Genesis and obvious reference (and mistake on God's behalf) that indicates that humans are all God's. They create their destiny and future. However, one thing that I will acknowledge is that humans are limited to existence (as an organism on planet earth). God and Lucifer are immortal (spiritually) while humans are immortal (spiritually but not physically). God and Lucifer are allegedly physically immortal if they choose to be; but humans only have one option (eternal spirituality). Still, the day that humans are superior in intelligence (we are getting closer) than today, God (the entity) will no longer be worshipped by his servants (slaves). God desires slaves and servants. Mankind desires to serve no one except themselves and they're self-pleasures; because, this is what

20

manifests their greatest happy and rejuvenation. I also do notice that this most sacred and often overlooked biblical verse never acknowledges that God directly speaks to Adam and Eve with Lucifer as the only witness, that...

"And the lord God said, "The man has now become like one of us (God), knowing good and evil. He must not be allowed to reach out his hand and take also from the tree of life and eat, and live forever." – Genesis 3:22

God knew that humans would be a threat to him; and since Adam and Eve acquired his (God's) knowledge and wisdom, they can never acquire the chance and/or permanent opportunity of eternal (physical) life. Can you imagine if humans ever discovered this "Tree of Life" and ate from it? I can guarantee that humans, upon never experiencing death, would never believe in any Heaven or Hell; and thus would never believe in God or fear him (as God desires most) again. The word God in the dictionary would cease to exist; and atheism, nihilism, and Luciferianism, (maybe Buddhism because of its connection to the Doctrine of Attraction) would be the only religion or religious philosophy on earth.

So the lord God banished him from the Garden of Eden to work on the ground from which he had been taken. – Genesis 3:23

If Lucifer had the opportunity, as he already had his motivation, to escort Adam and Eve to eat from the "Tree of Life," he would have helped Adam and Eve live eternally (in their physical being) not to make them suffer; but to make them immortal like himself (Lucifer) and God.

21

II

"Wisdom is a shelter, as money is a shelter; but the advantage of knowledge is this: that wisdom preserves the life; of its possessor." – Ecclesiastes 7:12

In the previous chapter, I discussed the basic concept regarding the Doctrine (law) of attraction. However, this chapter is dedicated to discussing the origin and/or the reality of its existence that is clearly visible (yet concealed for many reasons) in religious literature. The Doctrine (law) of attraction is and will always be a physical, yet invisible energy that responds to both our positive and negative feelings with or without our knowledge of knowing this. What is the response that the universe is giving to you based on your feelings and/or emotions? What feelings and/or emotions (whether good or bad) are you transmitting to the universe so that the universe can respond no differently than a person returning a missed-phone-call from a friend and/or relative? The Universe operates in a similar fashion. What you do or don't want, or whatever you think about or desire so much with a burning desire and passion, the universe knows. It, (the universe) only knows because it reads your thoughts like a professional medium. The universe has that psychic ability to know what you think and feel. No human being on earth can lie to him or herself; and most certainly, you cannot lie to the universe about your feelings and/or emotions. God (a divine entity) is not the one responding to your feelings

22

and/or emotions. You, as a human being, are attracting what you are giving (your brain frequencies of feelings and/or emotions) because you, yourself, are your own God. You know what you think and feel! You know if you feel good or bad! The Universe also knows because it is an organism that also has the ability to have feeling, ingenuity, wisdom and life. The Universe is a living thing; as you are. While you submit your brain frequencies to the universe of how good you feel; or better yet, how great you feel and desire to continue feeling more great, you are calling on the universe that works every day for your advantage (and disadvantage for those negative thinkers), it is always missing your phone-call to them. However, just because it is busy and is getting ready to prepare your next destiny in your future, does not mean that it will not return your call. The universe is required (by law) to return your call when the time is necessary for it to come. How quickly that you desire your cell-phone to ring (knowing it's the universe calling you to render a judgment based upon your feelings and/or emotions) is based upon your desire or passion on top of your feelings. The phone call (the universes response to your feelings and/or emotions) can take less than twenty-four hours, or perhaps a little over twenty-four hours, or maybe even a week, or perhaps longer, or perhaps shorter. The time-length of receiving a phone call from the universe is based on how passionate you are about your feelings. For example, let's say that you don't want to run into traffic anywhere & everywhere you go driving inside your vehicle, more than likely, if you keep having this persistent thought of not wanting to experience traffic on the road, the chances are very high that you will experience a brief time or perhaps a long day of being stuck in traffic. Normally, the freeway that you take is

23

always empty regardless of the time and/or hour; but for some strange reason the freeway that you are using to drive to get to your destination is stuck in a heavy traffic-jam. Oddly, before you even decided to take this route instead of driving through the empty streets, you kept constantly thinking either with fear or a strong desire of not wanting to be stuck in traffic for your own apparent reasons. Let's say that you are running late and you desire no more obstacles from getting to your destination. If you would only change your mind and have a burning desire of repeating in your mind frequently, 'I want to get to my destination quicker' instead of 'I don't want any more set-backs' the two will differ and the negative one will overpower the positive because your choosing to select the mentality of not wanting to experience something because you do not like it. Remember, as I said in my previous chapter that when you constantly think about what you don't want, the universe is only responding to your feelings and/or emotions; the universe cannot nor does it determine which of your feelings is good or evil; or more desirable than another feeling. Remember, the universe is not here to judge your feelings and/or emotions; it is here to respond to your requests and/or wishes. The Universe is Universal therefore consisting of only one energy (entity); although it is single, it applies to every species (especially humans) on planet earth. This is why every human being is capable of attracting anything (positive or negative circumstances) at any time in their life because we are all connected to each other in this universe.

"I am the Lord, and there is no other; apart from me there is no God. I will strengthen you, though you have not acknowledged me." – Isaiah 45:5

24

This quotation above this paragraph is very interesting if not intriguing; because it demonstrates that God (You) is only one. Indeed, there is no other God but you. This also includes the Universe because it is also God. The universe is one God; because it responds to every human beings feelings and/or emotions based upon they're their wants and don't wants. The single universe knows what we are thinking and desiring; as well as what we dislike; and hate with our hearts and mind. That is the God that is mentioned in the book of Isaiah. Certainly, it is not logical to think that multiple Gods (angels and/or demons) control our destiny for us based upon luck. In that case, I imagine that most people on earth are very unlucky human beings; most never really satisfied with their lives or current affairs. While the Universe may put favorable and unfavorable circumstances throughout our life which is based upon our feelings and/or emotions, we all have the power and control to only request from the Universe positive circumstances and events throughout our lives. In a way, it is like a restaurant-menu that is asking what we would like to order. We are the clients while the restaurant-menu is exactly the Universe. What we select on the restaurant-menu will be created by the Universe and delivered to us like a waiter or waitress giving us our food. Have you ever noticed the 'specific' kind of friends and people you frequently encounter or have attracted throughout your life? No matter how much you may disagree that you are the same as those people still in your current lives, you are relatively the same as them. Your interests, goals, desires, dreams, and/or wants and don't wants are identical; and therefore the universe has placed these people by choice (your choice) in your lives. For example, do wealthy people spend more time with wealthy people or middle-class

25

people? Do drug-addicts spend more time with vegetarians or other junkies? Do gangbangers spend more time amongst themselves or with people that are political and care about the environment? I don't have to answer these questions for you to realize these answers. The wealthy person frequently thinks of happy thoughts, healthy living, prosperity, wealth, abundance, joy, love, respect, charity... these feelings and/or emotions are all positive; even wealth. Money is not a negative element. Money can be negative for some people but it is also positive to some people. All wealthy people see wealth as just another form or reason to be happy. The wealthy people also understand that feeling good and thinking good, is necessary to establish prosperity throughout their life with or without money. These wealthy people are also interested in meeting or coming across people who think and act like themselves. Wealthy people must surround themselves around luxury, prosperity, and abundance to encourage them to continue thinking the way they do; which is feeling good and thinking good. Wealthy people also understand the concept of exercising their body and mind; either through running, jogging, playing gold, playing tennis, and/or meditating. Exercising and taking care of the body; helps maintain your prosperity because you are taking care of yourself. You love yourself enough to take care of your body with exercise. When you love something or someone, the universe will respond with anything relevant to the word 'love' and will deliver your request to you in due time depending on how bad you desire it and/or want it. When you are exercising, the universe knows that you are attempting (with or without knowing) to request more relevant positive and/or exciting circumstances in your life because of your likes, wants and/or desires to take care of

26

yourself because your heart is dedicated to helping you improve your physical and/or spiritual well- being. Since you are a God, and you are requesting the universe to respond to you (with or without knowing) by granting your wish to be more healthy and happy with yourself, you will inevitably receive what it is that you are working hard for; on the condition that you are passionate about what you are doing. You must always love yourself and think that you are a tremendous and beautiful person inside and outside; regardless of what you previously believed or still believe till this very day.

"The faith that you have, keep between yourself (God). Blessed is the one who has no reason to pass judgment on himself for what he approves." –Romans 14:22

This verse is extraordinary because not only is it revealing a sacred text that confirms the Doctrine of Attraction; but it is also confirming the necessary ingredient (faith) and not to feel bad or any doubt or any selfishness on our behalf; in order to receive whatever it is that you want in life. Yet, many who have read this text tend to overlook it with or without (subconsciously) knowing. This text basically guides its readers to constantly keep the faith (in themselves) after desiring whatever it is that they (you) strongly desire. One may still read this unique verse in the bible and still not be convinced of its direct meaning to the Doctrine of attraction. So, to convince you, that you are your own God and the Doctrine of attraction does indeed exist in one of the most sacred pieces of literature ever written (yet concealed of its true meaning), and recorded strictly for another purpose; to keep the public dependent on only one God (not themselves) and to live their lives based on fate (luck), and not faith (belief in yourself). Here

27

is the perfect example in the Gospel of Mark (The New Testament) of Jesus himself saying this very special (yet obvious) reference to the Doctrine of attraction. This cannot be overlooked and ignored...

"Everything is possible for one who believes." – Mark 9:23

This is a quick easy reference to have un-denying faith in yourself along with the belief to acquire anything on this planet. Jesus understood this very clearly. Hence, Jesus himself walking on water. The basic story goes that Jesus's disciples while on a boat, before dawn, saw Jesus walking on the lake (with his feet above the water). While it is possible that Jesus had supernatural powers, it is also possible that everyone on earth contains the supernatural powers that he (Jesus) possessed himself. Obviously, before dawn (the sun is just about getting ready to rise) his disciples were panicking when they saw their son of God (Jesus) walking on the lake without sinking or drowning. Jesus didn't even have to swim. All he did was walk as if gravity did not exist underneath him (or in his world). Jesus was able to manipulate gravity because he understood the concept of the Doctrine of attraction. His confidence and faith in himself to be, do, or achieve anything and everything was superior to those around him. His level of confidence had no limits. Jesus also wanted to install this confidence upon everyone. However, Jesus knew that if humans once obtained this high level of consciousness that he (Jesus) possessed, than in the future mankind could and would inevitably evolve into selfishness. To fix this, he mentioned to his disciples the following quotation that for this quotation alone, every human being on earth who read or will eventually read this evil bible-verse should disregard the following biblical reference...

28

"Truly I say to you, it is hard for a rich man to enter the Kingdom of Heaven. Again I say to you, it is easier for a camel to go through the eye of a needle, than for a rich man to enter into the Kingdom of God." – Matthew 19:26

Always remember this; the Kingdom of Heaven and the Kingdom of Hell exists here on planet earth. The kingdom of Heaven consists of a life filled with happiness, abundance, prosperity, joy, love, and faith in yourself to continue to use the power of the Doctrine of attraction in order to receive whatever it is that keeps putting a smile across that beautiful face of yours. The Kingdom of Hell also exists as well. It is for the people who have doubt in themselves to succeed and achieve their personal agenda, goals, and/or dreams. These people can also have more anger, frustration, rage, hate, envy, jealousy, and issues with themselves and other people. As a result of all this negativity, these people are stuck in a world (a cycle within themselves), that is contrary to happiness and prosperity. Only one person helped these people establish one or both of these kingdoms into their lives; themselves (you). I must admit that whatever bad thing that has ever happened to me (the author of this book) is my own fault. All my faults and failures are my fault. All my losses are my own fault. All the jobs that I ever got terminated from are my own fault. The women that I have had relationships with in the past and have been engaged too, are my fault as the result of our devastating break-ups. If I am poor or have insufficient funds in my bank-account, that is because it is my fault. If I am unemployed, it is my fault. If I am sick (either mentally or physically), it is my fault. If I am angry it is my fault. I am the one responsible enough to control my emotions. If I lose control of my emotions, then I am at fault. This also applies to my accomplishments and success

29

in life. This happened because it was my fault. I had un-denying faith in myself to achieve and/or accomplish anything in my life. All my previous failures and/or losses are a result of my doubt (faith) not fate (luck). When I lost confidence in myself that I could achieve something in my life, I got what I didn't want. I became my own worst enemy. Why would I become my own worst enemy by doubting myself? Better yet, why would you (the reader) be your own worst enemy by doubting yourself? Why would you not have high self-esteem enough in yourself, to believe in yourself, and to accomplish, and conquer your own goals and/or agendas? Nothing can or will stop you from achieving your desired dreams and/or agenda! No matter how much you believe that your God (divine entity) has a plan for you, I assure you that that plan is pure default (an automatic alternative agenda for you if you fail to achieve your desires). Living life by a default program comes with both fortunate and misfortunate circumstances. However, living life by focusing and concentrating on your dreams, with a burning desire, and being patient for the universe to give you your request, is much more beneficial than living by a life that is pure default. You must always believe, that the world can never deny your requests and/or demands. The universe, by its own laws, are required to grant your every wish; how or in which way it comes to you, is not for you to decide. However, your only requirement (according to this law) is to focus and concentrate frequently on what you desire, need, want, and cannot live without in this life. Then and only then, will the Universe give whatever it is that you desire. The universe has no limits in regards to its generosity whether it comes to you individually or in bulk. Your brain frequencies cross with the Universe's signals because we are energy as the Universe is also equally.

30

YOU SHOULD AND MUST ALWAYS HAVE CONFIDENCE IN YOURSELVES...

YOU MUST ALWAYS LOVE YOURSELF...

YOU MUST ALWAYS HAVE FAITH IN YOURSELF...

YOU CAN BE, DO, HAVE, WHATEVER YOU DESIRE IN YOUR LIFE AND IN THIS WORLD...

YOU MUST NEVER DENY YOURSELF...

YOU MUST NEVER HAVE DOUBT IN YOURSELF...

YOU MUST NEVER LOSE FAITH IN YOURSELF AND GIVE UP...

YOU MUST NEVER GIVE IN TO FREQUENT FAILURE AND LOSSES... IN THE END, NO MATTER HOW MUCH YOU FAIL, YOU WILL INEVITABY BE THE CONQUEROR...

31

III

Take a look at these wonderful and beautiful doctrine of attraction quotes from the bible; this cannot be ignored! The evidence is clear; practice makes perfect. It's a fact; and when you desire to be good at something, it takes constant effort and practice. It cannot be done overnight; but it can be done over time. Remember, you can do and be anything that you desire. There is nothing wrong with being an amateur; after all, all experts at their profession(s) or occupation(s) are experts that have evolved from being a simple amateur. Take for example, Simon Peter (Jesus's disciple). Simon Peter was an amateur as a disciple, and a beginner at understanding the Doctrine of attraction. When you practice the Doctrine of attraction constantly and see it with your own eyes, whether you are inside of your home or outside in the world, you know it works because your thoughts have delivered your brain frequencies to the universe and as a result you have received a response back from the universe. For example, let's say that you lost your job, and you have been unemployed for a couple months, you are desperate for a job; however, you are desperate for a specific job. Almost all day and all night, all you have been thinking about for the past three days are wanting a job, needing a job, and having a job. All these feelings and desires are relevant to each other. Now let's say that out of

32

the blue, your friend calls you up on the phone or through your social network; and wants to treat you out for a nice lunch. You did not expect this call because you know your friend generally works on a Monday; but for his or her own reason, he or she took the day off and thought of you. He or she wants to enjoy his or her day off while having some lunch with you. So, once you get a call from your friend and are stunned or shocked to hear that your lovely friend has taken the day off and wants to spend time with you. After doing all those job-searches all weekend and still not receiving a call today (Monday), you decide to take the day off for yourself and have a friend's night out. You get ready; look great, feel great, and you are ready to have fun. Your lovely friend and you decide to grab lunch at a nearby mall. Upon entering the mall, before you go on the lowest level where the food court is, (you are on the highest level in the mall) you and your friend are walking towards the escalators (on the other side of the mall closer to the food court) that leads towards the lower level food court; when you notice that there is an event going. As you walk closer towards the event, you see multiple tables in a circular position but with different signs, advertisements, and people representing those tables dressed in different business attire; without even looking to see what the signs or advertisements say. You naturally assume since it is a shopping mall that these are independent sales business and/or agencies. However, as you walk closer towards the event (which is the closest way to get to the escalator and/or elevator to the food court), you begin to read the signs and advertisements listed on some tables. Many people are lined up at various tables. You notice, as you pass by, that the tables do not have any merchandise on the tables; only pens and paper. You still are not reading or

33

looking at any of the signs and/or advertisements on the tables or around the tables or the walls. Suddenly, your best friend nudges you from the side and says the following words to you: "I have been here many times in my life, I have never, ever, seen a job fair here in my life. They got a lot of different business's hiring here; maybe you should apply at one of these places. Most of the signs here say full time with benefits. I mean, you are looking for a job. Maybe if you like, after we eat, we can go back to your house and you can change clothes; and we can come back here." You begin to think to yourself, that's a very good idea; considering the fact that you are finally beginning to see what all the different signs say at the tables, "interviews guaranteed today! Apply now! No experience necessary, one interview only for the job." While you do not yet understand what exact type of business you will be interviewing with, (retail, office, Restaurant) you do have confidence in yourself that you can at least get one job. Especially, if some signs at the job fair are saying "Interviews Guaranteed!" Let's say for example, that you go back home after a quick lunch, get dressed in professional attire, grab a copy of your resume and/or cover letter in your portfolio, and you head back to the mall to the job fair/event. Then, after interviewing with three companies (human-resources agents sitting at the tables), you get a call back the next day saying that you are hired and you're going to start your new job in a retail store that's full time (not seasonal) beginning with your orientation on Thursday. Funny, how life works out. Was this a coincidence or a stroke of luck? In life, there are no coincidences. We make anything and everything appear in our lives based on our thoughts, feelings, emotions, and fear. You're brain transmitted energy (brain

34

frequencies/signals) to the universe, asking it for a job. The universe was able to determine your feelings on how bad you wanted it, needed it, craved it, desired it and finally, with our confidence so high, expecting it! The truth is, when you want something in life so bad, you have to reach out for it; and despite the many obstacles and/or failures that you may (or will) encounter, it is not a sign by a stroke of fate, that it is not meant for you. Only you know what is meant for you. For example, let's say that you have epilepsy, and every now and then you get a seizure. Common sense, along with compassion for your fellow humans (based on your condition), tell you that it's probably not best or ideal for you to continue pursuing a career in (piloting) or attempting at least to pursue a career to become a pilot for a major airline corporation. Although, piloting may have been your dream and/or ambition since you were a child after seeing an airplane fly in the beautiful blue-sky above you, you know that even if your physician declared you epileptic free for seven years, and you were now able to get a license to operate an airplane, you know that if you have a seizure on the job (or on your own free time) and you have a seizure, lives can and will be at risk. So in this case scenario, you know that the job for pilot is not right for you. However, the scenario that when you try to do something that you want so bad, like say, open your own business; but you keep getting denied loans in order to open your business because of your credit and/or debt-to-ratio income, you begin to wonder with those normal (yet evil) thoughts and/or feelings of doubt. Is this even right for me? What am I doing? My credit inquiries are only making my credit more worse and now I will have to wait even more longer (after getting denied by all loan agencies) to rebuild my credit.

35

Why am I even wasting my time? I'll just get a job somewhere else, work for them, make that business wealthier; and maybe if I'm lucky in a couple years, I will get promoted to some management or human-resources position. It is thoughts like this that will make you watch everybody else succeed and make you wonder to yourself, why can't I achieve the same thing? You can achieve the same thing. It may take many times to be able to finally succeed. It could only take a few. It all depends on your feelings, emotions, confidence, burning desire, and the necessity of not being able to live without your dream and/or ambitions. But when we are met with obstacles and we are being prevented either through circumstances and/or episodes, you are only being temporarily defeated from your success and destiny on whatever it is that you desire. Many people intend to think from their perspective and opinion that "if it's meant to be, it's meant to be!" When you have this mentality (which is probably as a result of having a belief in a specific religion), you are allowing your God to determine your future and destiny for you; and while you may pray to him or think on-and-off on what you desire and badly want, it is really the same as purchasing a lottery ticket and relying on fate to give you money. This is very different from having faith in yourself that you can achieve anything and everything that you desire, want, and need. When you rely on fate, you are not confident enough in yourself to believe that you will automatically win by scratching that lottery ticket. You believe if you win, that you won by luck. If luck does exist, which can never be proven (yet most of the population have faith in it), than I assume and can prove that most people are generally unlucky and are determined by fate to work for the rest of their lives as a middle-class average citizen. I am going to

36

use The United States of America (not the entire world) as my perfect example. In the USA, the population, according to www.census.gov/popluck/, is 318.9 million citizens as of 2014. Note: this does not include any undocumented citizens. Now with almost 319 million Americans and also including undocumented citizens, according to this massive population, The United States of America, at least according to CNBC, and its alleged statement that the United States of America is home to more millionaires than anywhere else in the world. According to its inquiry and its statement regarding the general population that are millionaires, as of 2014, it is estimated at around 10.1 million. This is the link for the article released by the author and confirmed by CNBC http://www.cnbc.com/id/102489739.

This article was published on March 10, 2015; which is the same year as this book publication; which is only fair to say that more millionaires could have been added to the population in addition to the already 10.1 millionaires in The United States of America. However, let's say that there are only 10.1 million Americans who are millionaires in today's population; the rest of the population are either upper middle-class, middle-class, lower middle-class (poor) or like Donald Trump who is just too damn wealthy.

NOTE: The population of The United States of America is 319,000,000 (estimated), which leaves only ten million Americans as millionaires.

319,000,000-10,000,000

The result is 309,000,000

And the rest of the population, where does that leave them?

37

Before we get to that question, let's check out this intriguing yet alleged accurate article published by NBC News http://www.nbcnews.com/business/economy/number-billionaires-hits-record-high-2014-thanks-u-s-n205131

In this article, NBC is admitting that in a defaulting economy, for some strange (and not surprising reason) that billionaires are also increasing like-never-before in the United States of America; in fact more than in any other country. I can believe that for one reason alone; that I will explain later in the following chapters. But first, let's look at the population of billionaires in America. According to this article, The United States of America is home to 2,325 billionaires (increasing by 7% from 2013 to 2015). This, of course, is just an estimation. However, if there are only 2,325 billionaires in America (not including the rest of the countries on planet earth) than these billionaires know something that the rest of us do not. I am not a billionaire; I am not even a millionaire. I admit and acknowledge that; but at the same time, I also acknowledge that I choose to be that way at least for the time being. If less than 1% of the population in the entire world are billionaires, do you really think that this is an accident? Do you believe that these people are blessed with good fortune and God personally selected these billionaires to be blessed because God personally favors them above all others? No! God does not favor these people to become wealthy or the ten million Americans compared to the 308 or 309 middle-class or poor Americans. By the way, I determine middle-class Americans making an average of $60,000-120,000 (due to inflation) to be considered middle-class. Anything more that is made, in my opinion, is above middle-class into the higher middle-class. Still, I do not consider higher middle-class civilians to be wealthy. A wealthy person,

38

from my perspective, makes a minimum of $3,000,000 million dollars a year in income (after taxes). So what is the secret to these wealthy Americans who make millions of dollars a year? Are they blessed? Are they hand-picked by almighty God himself to distribute them wealth? Bullshit! These wealthy people, in fact, all wealthy people know a secret that they (this very unique elite) know amongst themselves but will not distribute it themselves out of fear of other competitors willing to take away the wealth from these wealthy Americans. Andrew Carnegie is credited to be the first (and one of the very few) wealthiest human beings in The Unites States; to reveal his "Sacred Knowledge" of wealth to his most trusted messenger, Napoleon Hill. It should be noted that John D. Rockefeller (Founder of Standard Oil Corporation) is to this very day, considered to be the most wealthiest American since the founding of The United States of America. With an estimated net worth of $336 billion dollars (in U.S. dollars today), he obviously conquered his ambitions in which he once reportedly said, "My two great ambitions are to make $100,000 dollars, and to live 100 years. Obviously, he accomplished his first ambition; John Rockefeller stopped at nothing no matter how the obstacles he faced to become wealthy. The same goes for Thomas Edison who failed over a thousand times to invent and make his invention work (the light-bulb). Imagine if Thomas Edison gave up his attempt to invent something that is still beneficial to humanity to this very day? No longer do we have to rely and use candles for our illumination at night. If luck does exist, obviously luck came to Mr. Edison 1,000 times after he failed. I admit and say to my readers that luck is an illusion. Our mind is what determines our ambition and agenda. In 1898, Henry Ford, being (at one point working

39

*with Thomas Edison himself) decided to establish his own
independent corporation entitled: The Detroit Automobile
Corporation. Mr. Ford failed with his newly established
corporation and was officially dissolved in 1901. Did this
stop Henry Ford from establishing a motor vehicle that
would be beneficial towards mankind? Obviously not, since
he is credited with establishing the assembly line for his
Ford Model T. It may have taken years to see some
progress; but eventually, his Ford Model T was introduced
to the public for the first time on October 1st, 1908 about
ten years after Henry Ford failed with his attempt in 1898
to successfully establish a motor vehicle; despite the
monetary donations from wealthy donors like William H.
Murphy and Thomas Edison himself. It may have taken
days, months, years, and almost a decade; but sometimes
that's how long success takes to occur; and inevitably it
will occur no matter how much time you may have to wait
for that success to appear. Failure can turn into success
just as easily as success can turn into failure overnight. As
I was demonstrating earlier, the second most wealthiest
man ever recorded in the history of our country was and
still is Andrew Carnegie; yet Mr. Carnegie was generous
enough to release/reveal his "Secret" of wealth to
Napoleon Hill so that the general population (poor or rich)
can have the opportunity of becoming wealthy if they abide
by certain conditions and use their brain to manipulate
their minds by convincing themselves that success is
inevitably and doubt is not tolerated. Indeed, what is the
point of believing that you will succeed and prosper if you
still have doubt that you are not lucky as rich people who
have no concerns about paying their bills, eating, having a
roof under their head, etc? You must convince yourself that
no matter how much you fail or think that you will fail, that*

40

you will succeed; even if you have to experience and/or see the worst that you would never imagine that you would face and/or experience in your life. When you have high-self-esteem in yourself, when you believe that you can, do, be, have whatever you want whenever you want, when you learn to love and appreciate yourself, and are convinced that you deserve whatever it is that you deserve, you will observe, attract, embrace, endure, and inevitably receive anything relevant to having a good life. It could either be that someone compliments your appearance and/or work ethic, it could be someone bringing you a gift and/or present, it could be someone sending you a positive message either through your cell phone, social network, or in the mail; it could even be a promotion, raise, a success towards your book and/or novel that you wrote; it could also be success in establishing your own business. Love and appreciation, must never dissolve within you; it must continuously be a cycle within you. The thoughts, emotions, passions, desires are in you; you must not lie to yourself. So what if you feel that you were not the most popular or handsome (for men) or most beautiful (for women) person in your high school, college, and/or work? You are beautiful and wonderful in so many other ways; that you must realize that you are for you to succeed. You must take care of yourself as well; you must love your body as you love your soul. If you hate yourself because you are not attractive, creative, talented, obese, and/or have diseases that the general population doesn't have, I admit that it is hard; but it is not possible. You must practice and find what positive and great advantages that you have that you know the general population does not have. You must believe that you are better than you think; that you are on top of the pyramid above everything and everyone else. It

41

does sound selfish! However, what is more selfish is convincing yourself that you are destined and designed to be at the bottom of the foundation while others are designed and/or meant to be at the top of the pyramid. You must rid yourself of any doubt within you; I will frequently mention to you many times throughout this book that doubt is your worst enemy; it is the most ruthless enemy that you will ever encounter. What's worse, is that it may follow you everywhere; but if you allow doubt to conquer your faith, you will see the results of unhappiness and/or misfortune. If you feel that you are a late-bloomer and you are angry and/or disappointed because you notice everyone else around you has far more luxurious opportunities, vehicles, and success in their lives, yes, you will feel left out. However, if you succeed and go above all those who were early-bloomers who barely had to lift a finger to find such a success, while you had to do more for less; you will have this powerful feeling that you are invincible; that you were at once, in the most poorest and vulnerable position; and all those who succeeded before you are now second, while you are above them; first and foremost. This does not mean that you should envy and/or have resentment against others. You should only think about yourself and decide what it is that you want to do; before you take action on whatever it is. For example, let's say that you desire to become an actor or actress, what will you do to make that happen before you fantasize, obsess, dream, want, and desire to happen? First, you should go to a professional photography studio and go with your best appearance (magnetizing attire, professional make-up, your hair nicely done) and take a couple of shoots. It is worth the fifty-to-hundred (maybe more) bucks. Again, no matter how you look, you must convince and acknowledge that you are a

42

naturally gorgeous super-star. Do not have doubt in your infinite beauty; secondly, it really depends on how or what you want to go about it. You can enroll at your local community college and/or university to attend drama courses, screen-play courses, acting courses, play courses, you name it. More often than you think, many of these instructors have connections to the entertainment-industry; if you befriend, respect, and dedicate time to your professor, you may humbly request (in the most respectful way) how to get in the entrainment industry; you may also request if your instructor, upon knowing that he or she are in frequent touch with agents, if they will pass your portfolio (containing your professional photos and resume) to the agent that has experience working with studios and well-known directors, producers, actors. If you do not want to go through all this trouble without first knowing how the entertainment industry is from the background there is never anything wrong with that. After all, you got to start somewhere; you can check to see in magazines, newspapers, online (Craigslist) to apply for "Movie Extras" you are pretty much guaranteed to be a movie-extra; and generally the pay is between fifty-to-three-hundred dollars; and you may even get free food (and parking). All that is required is that you follow directions from the director that is shooting; when he or she says the most infamous word "Action!" I highly suggest that if you do this second option, bring two books (your most favorite), a cell-phone charger (since most likely you will have your cell-phone with you), bring a friend if possible; and find any way to distract yourself from not being bored. Most importantly, volunteer (for free) your services to the director and/or people in charge of making, establishing, and or at the bare minimum the individuals responsible for

43

shooting the film. These people will appreciate your hospitality and generosity; and it is true, in life, nothing is free. Everything costs something to get something. But in the end, it pays off. Think of it like a job interview, you must spend money to get professional attire and/or resume paper, a printer, gas for transportation, even pocket-change for the parking meter. But in the end, is it worth it? Your rent is paid, you are able to buy food, pay your registration and car insurance, go out on a date with your lover, save money, and do much more. If you decide to be a movie-extra, while you may not be the main star of the attraction, know that your role is still important as a background person. You convince the public that the movie and/or show (or act) is realistic. Indeed, you may get paid less, may not be recognized, but you are still important. You are like one of the many wires that is able to light up the light bulb. And remember, Thomas Edison, a man who helped the light-bulb come into the world to be a positive luxury in every human-beings life, was dyslexic. Yes, he suffered from dyslexia but did that stop him? No, he succeeded, and so will you! No matter how many times you fail; you are one (or many) steps closer towards success; for every bad thing or negative opportunity and/or circumstance that occurs in your life, is for your benefit; and a lesson (wisdom) for you to learn not to repeat the same mistake. Failing is one thing; but giving up is another. Never give up on yourself! Otherwise, you may have prevented yet another beneficial resource and/or product that could, would, and will inevitably be beneficial to yourself and to mankind. Even if it doesn't involve discovering and/or inventing something, nothing is better than conquering your goals, motivating, and inspiring others to follow behind you... The Leader!

44

IV

"Whatsoever, ye shall ask in prayer, believing, ye shall receive." – Matthew 21:22

To this very day, I still cannot understand why God does not clearly spell out to his messengers, disciples, and/or prophets, the real method, reason, element, or way, of attracting anything and everything we desire. Here are other another biblical quotations that no doubt are references to the Doctrine (law) of attraction in the New Testament in the Book of Matthew:

"Faith is the substance of things hoped for, the evidence of things never seen" - Hebrew 11:1

"Whatsoever, things are true, honest, just, pure, lovely, of good report, if there be any virtue, or any praise, think on these things." - Philippians 4:8

"Ask and it will be given to you, seek and you will find, knock and the door will opened to you." - Matthew 7:7

"What things so-ever you desire, when you pray, believe that you receive them, and ye shall have them." - Matthew 11:24

As a Luciferian, you must rely and believe in yourself; your worship in another entity and/or religion will betray you, lie to you, and lead (and leave) you in directions where you will inevitably be lost; because you do not exactly know

45

what it is that satisfies your God. As a Luciferian, you are not worshipping the devil or Satan as some people think or associate Lucifer with such an alleged evil-entity. You are worshipping yourself; convinced without any doubt that you are capable of establishing your future with your own, powerful, belief-in-yourself. The great thing about being a Luciferian is that you don't have to be an atheist and/or devoted Christian to become a Luciferian. You can believe in anything that you desire or want; because what brings you eternal happiness is what matters (even if your happiness is selfishness to others perception); whether it be good or bad. Lucifer, the fallen angel who appeared to Adam (the honorable serpent) desired to give Adam enlightened intelligence. After all, what good was it for Adam and Eve to be born without any intelligence? Lucifer was the fallen angel who enlightened the very first human beings on earth. Remember, as I mentioned in the first chapter that God lied to Adam and Eve; that they would both die if they ate (yet alone touch the fruit) from the tree that is in the middle of the garden (commonly known as the tree of enlightened intelligence). So much for food poisoning right? It is interesting (and amazing) to know that there are different beliefs in the Luciferianism beliefs and/or religion. As a Luciferian myself, I cannot and will never acknowledge Luciferian as an independent religion; only a believing principle; of which I desire to occupy, use, learn, educate, and understand on my own terms. Luciferianism is a "belief" in individual supremacy. The ability to manipulate your own energy and mentality to receive everything that is in favor for you. But in no way, is this "belief" limited only towards the Doctrine of Attraction. In fact, the Luciferianism "belief" can probably be defined in my private dictionary as "belief" with

46

unlimited requests and/or opportunities for wisdom, intelligence, and/or knowledge. Fear does not exist in any Luciferian. Luciferians accept their successes and failures. Luciferians are not limited to general explanations that is generally perceived as accurate and/or valid; either by government and/or religion. Luciferians, as enlightened and open-minded conscious-beings seek more than just what is written, seen, heard, tasted, and feel (touch). Luciferians, desire, crave, and thirst on knowledge; answers are never enough to them. We do not believe in just one possible answer and/or way. We believe and always have faith in alternatives. We are not convinced and/or naïve of government and/or religion; as we both understand (either early or later in time) that both (government and religion) are the only two entities that subconsciously condone, endorse, encourage, and desire slavery for human beings. If you are a Luciferian, than you understand that slavery is not limited to chains around your ankles or massive debt tied to your legal name; which are condoned and allowed by religion and/or government. Currently, Niger and Sudan still allow and condone slavery; as well as The Islamic State of Iraq and Syria; as an example of slavery still condoned and treasured by selfish human beings. As a Luciferian, the liberation mentality is constantly in our minds. We believe that everyone, regardless of sex, race, color, religion, and/or sexual orientation should be able, and encouraged to seek open and/or hidden knowledge and/or wisdom. The opportunity for you to become wealthy (if that is your desire) should be for your own benefit. We do not believe as (Christianity and Islam) does that mankind should have limits. The Luciferian concept and "belief" is to assist others with knowledge and wisdom to their advantage; we

47

support everyone to fulfill their agendas of infinite self-pleasures. We are not submissive to any government, religion, and/or other human beings. If, however, we choose to submit ourselves to Lucifer as our supreme ruler, than that is our choice; but we as Luciferians, will not encourage (although we will accept) anyone to worship Lucifer. Although, to some Luciferians, (and non-Luciferians), Luciferianism is a religion. For example, in Theistic Luciferianism, some Luciferians acknowledge or at least believe that Lucifer is an actual entity, an educator (teacher), a guardian of mankind, and the true loving-spirit who enlightened mankind with infinite intelligence; which is often overlooked and ignored by government and/or religion. To Theistic Luciferians, Lucifer actually exists and may or may not be a symbol or myth of any kind. His presence is well known; and will forever walk all over earth. Some Theistic Luciferians, also will or will not necessarily join any church or place of worship to engage, pray, ask, seek, and or engage in séances with Lucifer for guidance (not necessarily to submit themselves to Lucifer). These Luciferians may be individual Luciferians or seek 'specific' friends and/or join them in worship; and not necessarily get involved with any other Luciferians for their own personal reasons. In this unique Luciferian religion (Theistic), magic and meditations may (more than likely) be involved; depending on deep you are into Luciferianism, this can either be seldom and/or frequently mediation and use of magic. Luciferians (of all kind) will always believe that God is not a friend or ally of mankind. Indeed, we are convinced that if God wanted everything his way, we would still be slaves without any intelligence and/or technology to help us improve and carry on with our lives. We do not mind spending our time condemning God. However, we

48

prefer spending more time to prove that mankind's only god is himself; and that pursuing intelligence and wisdom is never enough. More is required and/or needed for our times (the 21st century). We can never have enough of abundance; we crave, need, and thirst for more as a vampire thirsts for blood. Condemners and non-believers of Luciferians may protest and/or ignore the Luciferian belief; that we are Satanic worshippers; but this is far from the truth. If we choose to be a Luciferian and/or a Satanist; that is our selection of choice; and should never be disregarded as evil or inferior by any means. I generally believe that God symbolizes ignorance and stupidity while Lucifer symbolizes divine intelligence and infinite wisdom. This is the Luciferian philosophy! The ability to do, have, be, and want anything, no matter the quantity, and/or value is never selfish. What is selfish is not being true to yourself and denying your own happiness to an entity (that you can never truly satisfy or understand how to truly satisfy such an emotional creator). However, if I could and knew that mankind would be better off without any religion, (which I am convinced), and mankind would prosper and benefit without the need for Christanity, Catholicism, and Islam, I would do everything in my power to destroy all these religions and encourage (without force and invitation from enlightened-seekers) the principles and concept of Luciferianism. After all, my desire is to see everyone progress, succeed, and follow their own instincts without having or feeling fear of punishment from this lifetime (and the after-life) from an angry God. The fact that people have fear in such a God who apparently will not forgive them and make them burn in hell for eternity, should be enough for anyone to be convinced that God really does not care to see the human-species happy and content with they're their

49

self-pleasures. For example, if I am in love with a man (The author is a male), and I desire to marry or have sex with him; will I burn in hell just because of this clear and ridiculous warning in the (extremely) old Testament in the Book of Leviticus.

"And if a man lie with mankind, as he lay with a woman, both of them (the two men) have committed an abomination: they shall certainly be put to death; their blood is upon them." – Leviticus 20:13

So, I have to be executed, either by being beheaded, stoned, stabbed, shot, or burned just because I like and enjoy having sex with the same gender? Let's say the author is bisexual; and enjoys having sex with the same gender, I'm not going to explain what I desire in sex; but the point is, is that I have no fear nor do I care what others think of my morals and/or feelings. I do not care how offensive my desire to have gay sex is to people who condemn my, and other actions that I will inevitably engage in. As these are my choices and satisfaction; and if I desire this, I will have it. By that I mean, I was not born bisexual or gay; I was born straight! I wanted to have gay sex by choice; because sex is still the same (regardless of gender). I do not understand why people hate, dislike, and/or condemn homosexuals, bisexuals, trans-genders, or anything homosexuality related! However, I do know that such condemners and opponents that use biblical references to justify their cause for such opposition to human feelings and desires, always (under all circumstances) follow whatever they feel to follow. These hateful condemners do not want to see others happy; for fear that they either want to control (enslave) the general population to their beliefs, or these condemners believe that God, will once again,

50

become hateful, resentful, and will once again attempt to exterminate the human species or destroy the world and the rest of the other species combined. These people, the condemners (followers), believe and are convinced that they will suffer the consequences if they tolerate and/or allow same-sex marriage or same-sex couples engaging in sex. First of all, I understand that Adam and Eve were designed to procreate; but what I also understand is that God knew that if humans were given the privilege and opportunity to "love and have "feelings" than we will inevitably begin to love people of the same gender. I am convinced that homosexuality is natural; as well as having and engaging in sex with the same gender. Do you want to know why? Think about it! Men have a prostrate; and while men cannot get pregnant, when we engage in anal sex, (on the receiving in) we have something commonly called the prostrate; which means if we get penetrated; not only will men satisfy their penetrating partner, but through anal stimulation; and without the need to masturbate simultaneously while being penetrated; the receiver can experience a healthy and satisfying orgasm like-never-before. The prostrate allows for this to happen. Now, let's say that two men who are gay and do not ever engage in anal sex, oral sex is also the option and so is foreplay. By the way, those who commonly think and say the rectum is an exit-hole and not an entrance-hole, may also want to think that the mouth is generally supposed to be for consuming liquids and food as well as breathing air. It would not be fair for straight-couple condemners to say that anal sex is wrong but oral sex is okay. Both are satisfying and are practiced every-single-day by people. Why? Because, it makes them happy; and that is what matters! Having sex with the same gender can even be

51

(though not always) more satisfying than having sex with the opposite gender. For example, lesbians understand and know how to satisfy each other emotionally and sexually. I can admit that! In fact, most bisexual women admit or will admit (if asked) that having sex with woman is more satisfying than having sex with men. Why? Women have something called a clitoris; and when this is kissed, licked, sucked and/or gently massaged in a satisfying manner, women can successfully have the best orgasms. In fact, some lesbians consider this more favorable than being masturbated by their partner. Men only desire to penetrate; and while some may be generous enough to satisfy a woman's clitoris to the point of climax (achieving an orgasm), men will generally love to put their penis somewhere, in any hole. That is not to say that men are bad in bed; it's just an example and a fact! Women can be penetrated through the vagina and still feel satisfied but sometimes, not as satisfying as oral sex through their clitoris. Women do not have a prostrate; but can still feel somewhat satisfaction through anal penetration. Having sex with the same gender is natural; and it always will be. Sex does two things, as it has always intended to be; populate and satisfy the individual who reaches climax. If sex hurt before, during, and after climax; all the time for every human being, mankind would have been extinct a long time ago. People have sex; because it makes them happy. It is a self-pleasure and a natural desire. However, it is only natural for those who are legal (reach puberty) and of proper (legal) age. Luciferianism believes in self-pleasures and desires; and it does not count towards fantasizing on kiddy-porno or anything like that; as that involves hurting others; and Luciferianism does not condone and/or tolerate that. We tolerate and support

52

everyone achieving their desires and happiness without hurting others physically and/or emotionally intentionally. However, when we voice our opinion in protest and opposition from many, as Luciferians, it is our job and duty to continue voicing our opinions and rebelling against the status-quo (government, policies, statues, and religion). I am an advocate and supporter of same-sex marriage; and encourage it as well. I will be honest; I see it as natural; and believe that others should not have the right to tell others who to fuck or get married to. If I can serve your country and protect you from an invading country and terrorists (domestically or internationally) by enlisting or being drafted in the armed forces, and if I pay taxes, than I should be able to marry and fuck who ever I want, whenever I want; and I should get the same respect and benefits as opposite-couples receive. Although, I admitted that I do not mind being bisexual by choice, I do acknowledge and have always been convinced that others are born, select (choose), and become gay, lesbian, bisexual, transgender. If I was born gay, and I want to marry a man, I should have the right; and I will have that right; either by protest or by war. However, I have other desires. These are examples. Luciferians are not quitters; nor do they believe in defeat or submission. We believe that we are leaders and educators. We are the real messengers who speak and desire to reveal the benefitting truth to mankind for their sake; because it is the right, moral, honorable, and descent thing to do. When we allow religion to rule our lives; we are slaves. I have to admit that it's aggravating in countries like Guinea and Egypt, female-genital-mutilation (cutting off the clitoris so women cannot experience full sexual pleasure and/or climax) is still practiced; this is evil. If the clitoris is so unnatural, why

53

does every woman, who is born, have one? Why do men only have prostrates? Again, I ask these questions a lot; and I believe that I have the answer; because it is natural for us, as a human race, men and women, to have these sexual stimulators (clitoris and prostrate). Islam is mostly credited for the requirements (through the Tabith) to require women to have their clitoris removed. By the way, nowhere does the Quran mention the necessary removal of the clitoris for all women. It's interesting to know that the Tabith is not considered valid by some Muslims as the Koran; yet it is still practiced and required by some countries that are predominantly Muslim. I also do not find it fair, yet even credible, that God made men with prepuce (foreskin), and like the constantly changing of his mind, decides to threaten Prophet Abraham that if men do not get circumcised on the eighth day of life, Those sinners have failed to fulfill God's covenant. So, again, he wants us (human-beings) to believe that he created us from dust, but he wants us to alter our body parts because he suddenly changed his mind or made a mistake in creating us? Either one is the right answer. Again, this is why Luciferians generally ignore and/or do not worship God; while they (like myself) may acknowledge his existence; we do not submit to him; because he (God) is flawed and imperfect as I mentioned in the first chapter. God allegedly does not have limits as we do humans, but neither God or humans are perfect either. Perfection, is an illusion just like God. He is an illusion of justice, equality, fairness, charity, and everything that is directly and indirectly positive. That is false; because of his frequent prophets and messengers, the war on religion still continues to this very day. Do we really need pole-shifts, earthquakes, and tsunamis to depopulate mankind every day? No, because, religion does

54

the job that mother-nature does not have to do. The result, upon having religion has and always will be war; never peace. Peace is an illusion. Sins (self-pleasures) are more dominant than resistance (refusing to sin) because it is natural. Sinning is not just fun; but satisfying and entertaining. Whatever is generally frowned upon (but legal) to religion and others happens to put smiles on those sinners faces; because, it makes them happy. I wonder when the next Prophet comes, how many millions (or billions) of lives will be exterminated. God doesn't mind; if he truly has the power to stop this, why doesn't he? I find it so sad that people will ignore their happiness and desires based on fear from their "alleged" creator. I say alleged because, nobody can ever answer where we truly came from; and what is in the after-life. Does heaven have limitations towards happiness? Can I have sex in heaven with both genders? The real hell can be defined as ignoring everything that you desire and want because of your fear that God will never forgive you. Well, if there really is a hell, apparently, God doesn't forgive everyone and therefore is an emotional creator and therefore is imperfect; therefore does not deserve the Luciferian submission towards him (God) because an emotional thing or being cannot be trusted. Would you trust someone who changes his mind from time-to-time? 100% of the time, your reply is going to be "No!" I find it fascinating and genius that man has been convinced and perceived of the absurd "theory" that Lucifer is Satan and Satan is the enemy of humanity. Did God not grant Satan his title of authority over all the nations on earth and the most powerful general and authority in hell? Must humans suffer both in life and the afterlife because of their refusal to worship an invisible God that never speaks to you in this

55

*lifetime, never gives you advice, yet you pray to him
expecting, believing, and hoping that this entity hears your
requests, cries, and agony. I find it amazing that if your
schizophrenic and speak with yourself either because you
really are mentally ill or your energy is so sensitive to
other energy (spirits) that you have the unique psychic
ability to communicate with other beings from other realms
and/or dimensions, you are labeled an insane person; a
person who is the opposite of the average and ordinary-
sane individual who talks to himself (yet can justify his
reason for talking to himself by praying to his God).
Apparently, praying to an invisible God is normal and
sane; and even encouraged. However, if you are not
praying to God, and you are talking to yourself, you are
labeled a person who is likely mentally-ill (or under the
influence of drugs) and therefore must seek some form of
psychiatric treatment or rehab treatment. I often wonder
how many times God has failed to answer so many prayers;
because the bible does not acknowledge (admit) that men
and women are their own God's and creators of their
destinies. We are all connected to each other; good with
good, fair with fair, and evil with evil. While the arms and
legs of human beings are of such necessity and a valuable
asset towards every human being; as a necessity to survive
and accomplish duties and responsibilities; in my opinion,
the heart and brain are the most powerful muscle in every
human being. The heart contains emotions that are
transferred to the brain; and based upon those emotions
and/or feelings, the brain will unleash those emotions
(signals) to the universe; but God does not answer our
prayers because he suddenly feels like it. Again, we are
connected, so our thoughts must attract and inevitably
receive relevant and/or similar events, circumstances,*

56

and/or people to us within a short-time. We always get what we ask for and what we do not ask for. Everybody is connected with all of this. There is no such thing as opposites attracting each other; opposites of each other are similar and relevant to each other in unnoticed and unrevealed similarities. However, the "I Don't Want This" attitude is the reason why people attract and endure unpleasant circumstances and/or people in their lives and perceive this to be as opposites attracting each other. Intelligence attracts intelligence; and ignorance attracts more ignorance; peace attracts peace, while war attracts more war. I often wonder and have always been convinced that if so many human beings have been slaughtered, executed, beheaded, burned, shot, stabbed, blown to pieces, poisoned, boiled in hot water to death, and have received relevant torturous executions; for the accusation of being a heretic (sinner and unbeliever). It still continues to this very day and will continue if religion is not destroyed. Religion cannot be updated and/or altered to benefit its believers and establish peace on earth. At least with religion completely destroyed and exterminated, the only wars that can ever escalate and exist will be based upon the only other reason for enabling war to exist: politics! However, with religion and politics as allies and in control of the world, depopulation will never stop. Judaism is clearly outdated; yet still practiced. Like the Holy Bible and The Holy Quran contradicting itself over and over again, never really making full sense of its meaning and its requests from mankind; in a way, the first Amendment to The United States Constitution is similar. The first Amendment guarantees the right to practice whichever religion that is your preference; and Christianity (Protestants), being the primary, common, and dominant

57

religion in the United States, I will use this evil religion as a perfect example of justifying the extermination of its practice; without necessarily enslaving its followers as Christianity secretly does to its own followers. While the United States government advocates and practices freedom and democracy to some extent; (I say to some extent because of the current government's consistent disregard and disrespect to civilians civil liberties); nonetheless, we are free to practice and worship God; and to identify ourselves as Christians if we humbly choose to do so without any opposition. Yet, not every Christian will faithfully follow his or her own religion to its entirety. For example, former Founding Father, James Madison, (former President and author of the First Amendment) who was an opponent and enemy of King George III (King of England during the American Revolution) and who successfully assisted with securing American independence from England. As the father of the First Amendment, James Madison believed that people should not only have the right to religion but the right to free speech; something which contradicts each other to some extent. For example, in Judaism, saying "God Damn It" back in the day (and till this very day in some countries) would & will get you stoned. Yet, in this sacred Amendment, you are free to practice Judaism, and this religion requires you to stone blasphemers of God.

"Anyone who blasphemes the name of the lord must be stoned to death by the whole community of Israel. Any native-born Israelite or foreigner among you who blasphemes the name of the lord must be put to death."
-Leviticus 24:16

58

Yet, obviously, if you do stone a blasphemer like me for saying "God Damn It," you will be sent to prison before you get sent to Heaven (or Hell for violating the sixth commandment "Thou shall not kill," yet another contradiction). God cannot kill me himself immediately for condemning him; instead, he wants you to kill me; because, you are his follower (slave). If you refuse, you must be beheaded yourself because you allowed yourself to become a member (civilian) of a city that has gone astray from God. If you are a devoted Christian, would you believe that playing with the tarot cards and Ouija board is equivalent to practicing witchcraft? Should I be stoned, because, I desired to summon Lucifer or a spirit to guide me to the correct path for my own personal salvation and desires; or if I desired to know and prepare for a future that I can easily alter with my mind (law of attraction)? Back to James Madison, and let's include Thomas Jefferson (another former President and Founding Father) who was an advocate of civil liberties and frequently warned Americans about tyrannical government and abuse of power. Thomas Jefferson, like all the Founding Fathers, always warned the public never to submit to government or sacrifice liberties for securities; or fully trust the government all the way, to warning about rebelling against its government; in order to maintain and stabilize freedom and democracy from future tyrants and/or abusers of civil liberties and the Constitution.

"The tree of liberty must be refreshed from time to time (generation to future generations) with the blood of patriots and tyrants. It is its natural manure." – Thomas Jefferson

"If a law is unjust, a man is not only right to disobey it, he is obligated to do so." – Thomas Jefferson

59

"You Are God"

"No freeman shall ever be debarred (prevented) the use of arms. The strongest reason for the people to retain the right to keep and bear arms (have guns), is, as a last resort, to protect themselves against tyranny in government."
– Thomas Jefferson

Clearly, this enlightened Founding Father knew the threat of tyrannical governments; and perhaps we are living in the times of his accurate predictions; but that is a different topic and debate. I only use this example to justify this next biblical-text that clearly contradicts patriotism; and instead, encourages cowardly actions and submission to government as an alleged command from God.

"Let every person be in subjection (submit themselves) to the governing authorities. For there is no authority except from God, and those (government entities) which exist are established by God. Therefore he who resists authority has opposed the ordinance of God; and they who have opposed will receive condemnation upon themselves. For rulers are not a cause of fear for good behavior, but for evil. Do you want to have no fear of authority? Do what is good, and you will have praise from the same; for it is a minister of God to you for good. But if you do what is evil, be afraid; for it does not bear the sword for nothing; for it is a minister of God, an avenger who brings wrath upon the one who practices evil." - Romans 13:1-4

First of all, even if you do good deeds and somebody else is far more superior above you, either because of wealth and/or position of power, do you really think that you will be saved from execution from God because you knew in your heart you were innocent from the beginning? So clearly, the biblical-text above states that God selects and places whoever he wants, whenever he desires, in charge of

60

a nation or at the very least a land filled with population. Does God really expect the human population to submit themselves to a tyrannical government who chooses to nullify and abolish citizen's civil liberties and freedoms? Should we obey such tyranny? What is the reward besides humiliation, cowardice, and inevitably becoming a slave to another human being once we submit ourselves to tyrannical authority? Heaven? Does this sound like a caring God who cares for his people? Religious or not, every human being cherishes and loves freedom; it is a dream and reality. It may never be appreciated always, but it is always cherished when it is practiced. Freedom is just as natural as love. Yet, the bible forces people to relinquish their thoughts on liberties; and to submit ourselves to bullies and tyrants. Patriots are born every day in this world to help aid other patriots against tyranny. Not only did God allow Jesus to be whipped to death, but he also allowed Saint Peter (the first pope) to be crucified upside-down because Roman Emperor Nero believed that Saint Peter helped set Rome on Fire (which was false) and had Saint Peter executed. How does God allow people like Nero to roam freely around the earth is yet another question? I am convinced that since the First Amendment guarantees the right to practice any religion that you desire (even if it's self-made) but you are limited to its practices, than why should religion exist? The world does not need religion as the world does need government. As a Luciferian, we must always believe that if our rights are violated or abused, we shall never turn our cheeks as Christians through their cowardice, encourage and practice. We must rebel, punish, and exterminate all who practice to take away our rights, freedoms, and liberties. Future generations rely on our blood being shed. The general practice of Luciferianism is

61

believing and achieving our dreams and desires; without
worrying about any consequences and/or punishments.
There is nothing wrong with ignoring God and fulfilling
your self-desires; it is natural, moral, and right in your
heart, mind, and consciousness. Religion has never had the
right answer and it never will either; because there is too
many religions out there who contradict itself and each
other. Have you wondered why Judaism and Christianity
are different religions yet they're both included together
and titled "The Holy Bible?" It's because they're both the
same; and if you are not convinced, and you are a
Christian, Jesus confirmed it himself.

*"Do not think that I (Jesus) have come to abolish the Law
(the Old Testament) or the Prophets; I have not come to
abolish them but to fulfill (confirm) them. I tell you the
truth, until heaven and earth disappear, not the smallest
letter, not the least stroke of a pen, will by any means
disappear from the Law (the Old Testament) until
everything is accomplished." (Jesus) Matthew 5:17,18*

Now, let's look at Prophet Muhammad's proclamation;
(and contradiction) of Islam confirming the Torah and the
Gospels as equivalent to Christianity and Judaism through
the Archangel Gabriel (when he appeared to Muhammad to
remind him that Islam is no different from Christianity and
Judaism.). Although, Muhammad claims that Islam is a
separate and independent religion that should be
recognized and worshipped; and acknowledged differently
from Judaism and Christianity, he contradicts himself.

*"Anyone who opposes (Archangel) Gabriel should know
that he has brought down this (Quran) into your heart, in
accordance with God's will; confirming previous scriptures*

62

(The Torah and Gospels), and providing guidance and good news for the believers." – Quran 2:97

And after several thousands (and hundreds of years) later, the good news is (sarcastically and regrettably), is that people still die every day over the names Abraham, Moses, Jesus, and Muhammad; among others; but primarily Jesus and Muhammad; considering Christianity and Islam dominate the world as the two most common and popular religions. If inevitable death, turmoil, famine, thirst, hunger, imprisonment, torture, and more bloodshed will and must occur because of dead messengers and prophets alleged (but can never be confirmed) to be "messengers from God," than truly the extinction of the human race is possible (since humans are killed every day over these unreliable sources and theories from these messengers and prophets) and the only antidote to saving the human race and curing (not treating) the poison (religion) that is in itself evil, yet destructible, is exterminating all religions and practicing without prejudice and hatred towards each other, the concepts and doctrines of self-pleasures, wants, desires, and doing whatever it is that makes you happy. If religion makes you happy, by worshipping God, Jesus, Muhammad, Allah, Moses, Abraham, The Virgin Mary, or Buddha, or any other mythical God or deceased prophet, messenger, and/or prophet, I assure you that you can only hold in your temptations for so long; by refusing and ignoring your temptations to serve, worship, and obey your God, you will only witness temporary happiness; as you will always think (and never realize) whether you are actually satisfying your God. Your personal happiness matters; to be depressed, angry, sad, disappointed, nervous, scared, intimidated, worried, concerned, and betrayed are all the feelings that you're god wants you to

63

feel because he knows that you feel this way because whatever it is that you truly want is against your personal beliefs. If you desire to go drink or smoke because it makes you feel good, than drink and smoke. If sex makes you feel good, and your desire is to try sexual positions that are obviously offensive to your religion, still do what makes you happy. Your creativity is natural and normal; it is authentic 100% and when you ignore your self-desires, you are not yourself; you are a 100% artificial human being; who is afraid to be the real you! There is nothing to be afraid of! After all, God (the entity) will not pay your bills, put food in your mouth, put a roof over your head, pay your electric, gas, and/or water bill, your car insurance, your health insurance, your groceries, or anything else that you will inevitably pay because of your will and struggle to survive. Your brain and your two hands are what keeps you going; (and of course your legs). You can have all the confidence in the world and have everything in the world because you had faith in yourself; as I assure if you rely on fate (God) to deliver your personal happiness to you, I guarantee that you will be disappointed in your surroundings; even if you do not believe that you have the ability, power, and opportunity to determine your destiny and future. If you allow God to determine it completely throughout all your life, he will let you down when you least expect it. It is time that we all have to face, acknowledge, and accept all the rewards and consequences for our actions. For every positive action that we seek and carry out, indeed a negative thing lies ahead; as for every negative action that we seek and carry out, there is a positive thing at the end of its conclusion. As a Luciferian, the concept of understanding good and evil is not limited or really meant to worship or understand God or Satan;

64

rather, the enlightened concept is to educate all who acknowledge that for every decision that we make, it has its benefits and flaws; whether the decision is positive or negative. For example, if you sell your house; because you do not get along with your neighbors, you solved the problem of getting rid of your neighbors; but in the end, you are surrendering your house, which inevitably had at one point established positive memories; not just the negative (neighbors). While you move into another house in the same or different city and/or state, the new positive beginning is having a new residence; while the negative (temporary) beginning is having to adapt to the new town/city/state and/or country and learn the streets, area, grocery stores, etc. while that can be fun and interesting to some, to others it's the contrary; to others. Another positive circumstance or event is being a supervisor and/or manager; and having a great employee that works underneath your leadership. He or she makes you look really great to your own bosses; with the exception of one thing. He or she, is frequently ten minutes late either coming to work or coming back to work from lunch. You already have given several warnings; yet you do not terminate this employee because no other employee completes or concludes any of the required jobs better (or faster) than this employee & you know that if you terminate this employee, you will lose an irresponsible yet hard-working employee. Luciferians understand the concept that every decision and circumstance comes with both good and bad circumstances. A flaw comes with its many charms as many charms also comes with many flaws. Like the sun & moon, one controls the day and the other the night, this is balance. The morning star + evening star=Lucifer & Lucifer=enlightened intelligence for all from dawn to dusk!

65

V

"And, he shall separate them one from another, as a shepherd divideth his sheep from the goats. And, he shall set the sheep on his right, but the goats on his left." - Matthew 25: 32-33

Yes! In order to be a Luciferian, you must only be left-handed; that is the only requirement! Just kidding! Many (if not the majority), that I imagine, are probably right-handed; yet some Luciferians may follow (as Theistic Luciferians) a specific (yet unique) way of Luciferianism practice called "The Left-Hand Path." These Luciferians (Goats) seek or may attempt to practice either white or black magic for any purpose that they desire; including engaging in ritual magic just to speak or meet with Lucifer himself as an entity. These left-handers, while they may worship Lucifer; are generally not Satanists; since for the most part; Theistic Luciferians do not worship for the objectivity of evil; rather they may worship Lucifer to seek his aid or receive enlightened energy and/or inspiration. For the most part, however, Luciferians will either deliberately accept although (out of hatred and resentment for God) deny his existence; or some Luciferians, really do not believe in any God; but will acknowledge the sole existence of Luciferiansm; (believing that it is a concept to be practiced even if God cannot exist and therefore never created earth). One this is for certain, Luciferians are leaned more towards a rebellious yet intelligent, and

66

creative way of life. Anything and everything can be debatable and questioned; no matter how many answers are given as credible and/or a theory by any philosopher, author, and/or government. Luciferians are patriotic in their own way; yet many people who frown upon our philosophy think the opposite; that we are sinners that encourage, and support evil, and wickedness all because we refuse to follow these outdated book's (the Holy Bible and the Quran) teachings (first we would have to determine which religion is right) that obviously was designed, created, and established to enslave mankind; rather than help him become his or her own God establishing his or her destiny; with his confidence, ambition, desire, and creativity. I don't think that I am evil for telling people the truth; I probably have installed more confidence in my readers than most pastors and priests install currently any confidence whatsoever to its followers (slaves) at their designated churches. Remember, most pastors and priests will warn and threaten their followers (slaves) with frequent threats of consequences for sinning. According to the Holy Bible and the Quran, everything really is a sin. Even thinking of sinning without actually sinning is a sin. The only way to save yourself from burning in hell is to confess those sins; but even that doesn't really guarantee you eternal damnation; which is all just bullshit! I really believe that God lied about hell so he could have more people worship and submit themselves to him; because he knew that this threat of eternal damnation could convince his slaves to submit themselves to him. His method still currently works; because some people literally do worship him (for God's satisfaction) but never for their own satisfaction. Going back to the "left-handed path" philosophy or "way of life," I must mention the ever

67

magnificent Baphomet. Baphomet, (the goat headed entity or God) in any portrait and/or picture is generally a great representation and symbolization of the four elements (Water, Fire, Air, and Earth). Baphomet's wings represent the element of "air" while the torch above his head engulfed in flames represent the element "fire." The fish scale (near the black and white snakes) represent the element "water" while the ground-bump that he sits on represents the element of "earth." The light crescent moon next to Baphomets right horn (looking to our left side of him) represents "light" which is the symbol for positivity and anything that is good; while the dark crescent moon at the bottom of Baphomets left leg (looking on our right side of him) which represents "darkness" and symbolizes negativity and anything remotely bad. This, however, is an educated concept revealing that everything that is done or going to be accomplished and concluded, comes with both positive and negative attributes. Luciferians understand this concept that is necessary in order to carry out our personal self-desires and self-pleasures. Religion, on the other hand, like Christianity and Islam, define anything negative and dark as the arch-enemy of God; yet these stupid religions, which under-value human dignity and intelligence, declare that anybody who is on the left-handed path will never see the great "Kingdom of Heaven!" As a Luciferian, I make the choice whether I want to establish my own Kingdom of Heaven here on earth by learning, receiving, obtaining, and embracing forbidden knowledge and wisdom; and therefore creating my own destiny with my own mind and physical labor, or I can be negative and doubt myself of ever succeeding. If I fail to succeed, it's my own damn fault. If failure is inevitable, than we learn the positive outcome of failing, which is not giving up on our

68

dreams and ambitions; but acknowledging that we have discovered yet another method of failing in our attempt to succeed and now; we must not repeat the same mistake. That is the positive conclusion while the negative conclusion was failing. It is true that there is one way to make anything work (or perhaps many) to our advantage and benefit; and just because we accept defeat does not mean that the war is lost; only the battle. A Luciferian is equivalent to a soldier; a soldier learns new techniques and intelligence that he can generally never learn in the civilian world. Some things in the military are meant to be secrets; No doubt! Even in the civilian world, the same rules apply; for example, if you got a job at a bank issuing credit to clients; than inevitably you will understand how credit works and operates; and how it truly enslaves people rather than free them from debt. Credit is designed to put people in debt. Now, the creditor or banker knows the secrets of maintaining an adequate credit score suitable for future obligations (car, house, insurance); yet in the public-education-institutions, do you think that you will learn in high school, as a seventeen year old, how to establish and maintain positive credit in your name? After graduating, and upon turning eighteen years old (the legal age limit to obtain a credit card), do you know or will you know how to build credit even if your qualified and eligible to receive one from the greedy banks? The answer is no! Even if your desire is grad school, you will still never learn how to build and maintain your credit under your name unless you educate yourself by taking time out of your schedule to hit the books; and find out all the disadvantages that credit is designed intentionally to ruin your name. Yes, we are responsible for putting ourselves in debt, but the point that I am trying to make is it's a "secret" on how to build

69

credit. How about taxes? Do schools teach their students how to prepare themselves for the future on filing taxes in their name? This is another "secret" and it is designed to leave the American taxpayer ignorant of their earnings and filings. I do not intend to get political in this chapter; but again, I am using this as a perfect example of a Luciferian. Luciferians question anything and everything that doesn't make sense; and giving a kid a credit card to spend it without explaining to him how it works; is ruthless and tyrannical. One pleasant thing that all Luciferians share is the outmost concern for the general welfare of mankind; and this doesn't include the current generation but also for future generations. Prosperity for future posterity's is the mentality of Luciferians. Luciferians will only support any declaration of war from any government on the sole conditions of intent to free men, women, and children from either slavery of chains or slavery of debt; or the intent of defending anything defenseless against tyranny. You will never see a Luciferian praise a war that is based upon establishing wealth for a handful of assholes (please excuse my language) and leaving a massive deficit for their nation for the three letter word that is the primary justification (yet another secret from its government) for going to war, "oil!" This subject on a war-for-oil is something that Luciferians will find an interesting subject to discuss about; not because of their open-mindedness or their attempt to seek "forbidden knowledge" but because the anxiousness and ability to question something like a war-for-oil is extraordinary. Whether or not we go to war, it affects us all in some way (if we allow it). Another interesting subject that will no doubt include a debate (not fight) between Luciferians is this question. Why is it fair for any eighteen year old to pay taxes, get drafted to go to war and fight for

70

their country, obtain credit and ruin their name for many years to come, yet cannot have an alcoholic beverage until they're twenty-one years of age? Does that sound fair? If I was eighteen years old again, (I'm currently twenty-five years old) how is that I could put myself in massive debt, give away my hard-earned earnings (taxes) to the government, and even go fight to death for oil (not freedom) yet I cannot even touch a nice, frosty, cold-one (beer) after all the hard work of paying taxes (through physical labor) and serving my country (risking death). This is a perfect debate; because whether or not you agree that an eighteen year old should have a drink or be legal enough to drink, you may begin to think that all twenty-one year olds should be the new age of establishing credit, paying taxes, and getting drafted to go to war. If an eighteen-year-old is drinking beer, wine, and/or liquor, is not a great point in justifying my opinion that he or she who does all these for the government should be eligible to have a drink, consider this, In Las Vegas, if you're under twenty-one years old, good luck trying to gamble! Again, the government will let you go to war and risk death at eighteen; but if you don't believe in drinking alcohol; and you already have a credit card (since your eighteen-years-old), if you want to gamble in any casino in Las Vegas, unless you show up with a fake beard and a mustache, and wear a suit; you will just get escorted out. Unless your parents or family are staying at the hotel, even then, you still can't gamble. Does this sound fair? Apparently the big "21" is what gives your full freedom; while "18" only gives you partial freedom. It will never be surprising if Luciferians involve themselves in politics. Luciferians are open to anything; and while an ordinary person may think that "we" are weird and withdrawn because we believe in

71

certain theories that seem ridiculous; and therefore we refuse to follow the ordinary person and the "status-quo," we are proud of who we are. We are proud that we do not care what others think of us. This may be some indirect form of being rebellious; but in the end, it's what works. A sheep is a sheep; (ordinary civilians) and a goat is a goat (extraordinary civilians). Every Luciferian is extraordinary in their own way; whether they believe it or not; as I believe that if we follow everyone else and the status-quo, than we can never change the world that we live in. To change this world, for a more positive outlook and experience, one must rebel against the status-quo; it has been done throughout centuries and it will continue to persist. While Luciferians, perhaps a very, very, very, small portion probably intend to dominate the world for their benefit at the expense of other human beings through monetary gain and more land that is conquered, this does not mean that all Luciferians believe in this concept; while we would accept any Luciferian who desires wealth and property in bulk and quantity, we will support these self-pleasures and self-desires, but we will not tolerate injustice against our fellow human-beings such as war-for-oil. For example, if we do not agree with homosexuality; that does not mean that we should deny brotherly-love (or sisterly-love) to our fellow men and women that breathe the oxygen that the trees (not God) produce every day for the necessity of our survival. Since Homosexuality is becoming more common and normal (which it is in my opinion), we should encourage everyone not to hide or deny their sexual orientation; and befriend those who are only satisfying their own self-pleasures and self-desires. That is more courageous than holding it in and denying yourself. Coming out of the closet (revealing your sexual

72

*orientation) is the hardest thing that men and women have
to go through every day; and while some may hold it in
because they're embarrassed and/or afraid of being an
outcast from their family and friends, either temporarily or
permanently, these people deny themselves because "they
care what others think about them!" In a way, it's the
opposite of being selfish; you're afraid to hurt others
because of your sexual orientation; and while you may
prevent everyone from knowing the real you, you are only
hurting yourself because you refuse to satisfy your own
desires and pleasures. That is not fair; as I will continue to
remind the reader that it is crucial and a necessity to "be
yourself!" You may have heard that quotation by rapper
Tupac Shakur, "Only God can judge me!" While I admire
this talented artist with sincere respect and sympathy for
him, I disagree with this quotation. First of all, I am God;
and so is everyone else! I'll judge myself accordingly.
However, God himself, the man responsible for allowing so
much bloodshed to occur under his name, he (God) has no
right to judge anybody. The way that I see it, is that I did
not ask to be born; therefore all the positive and negatives
things that I do on earth are the result of me being here on
earth and doing whatever I see fit and makes me happy. If
God had it his way, we wouldn't even have a 7-eleven
today; we would still be wiping our asses with banana leafs
instead of toilet paper. We would not be served; rather, we
would be his servants. No Luciferian is a servant! We get
served; which means that when we get served, it is all our
dreams, ambitions, destiny, hope, and desires in bulk and
quantity! To other religious fanatics, this may sound selfish
as we are not serving God, only ourselves. However, there
is nothing ever wrong with spoiling yourself like a king or
queen; it is not only natural; it is also an obligation!*

73

VI

The Final Chapter

The greatest thing about being a Luciferian, is the ability to express your true-self. As I mentioned previously in this book, you cannot be completely and truly free in life, if you are convinced that God controls your destiny and fate. If you believe that you have no control over your life, regardless of the positive and/or negative circumstances against you, you will never be emancipated throughout all the years of your life. You and you alone, with your creative mind and your emotions, along with your actions, is the greatest and strongest weapon (tool) to carefully engineer the greatest discovery and invention (your destiny); that has no limits and all the infinite possibilities that you are capable of establishing. Remember, fear and doubt, are your two worst enemies. While both feelings are natural to every human being, fear and doubt, are the feelings to always disregard and avoid. God desires his humans to feel this way because he knows that people that have fear and doubt are his true & only followers (slaves). However, as God changed his mind from generation to generation, so have human beings; as we ourselves are God's. Truly, Lucifer is both a spiritual and actual entity; whether he lives in our world or in a different realm and/or dimension; his wisdom and knowledge is influential and

74

inspiring to mankind. One great thing about Lucifer (the entity) is, he has never betrayed himself; and has persisted his belief (if the Holy Bible and the Holy Quran are correct) that he is above all; and not inferior to anyone. He will not even recognize the alleged creator of the Universe to be above him; since Lucifer, after being removed from heaven, (if true) has established his Kingdom here on Earth. Lucifer has never deceived himself; as he is convinced that he has and deserves all the power that he needs to get which is his every desire, wish, and request. Without him, Christianity, Catholicism, and Islam would not even exist; as these religions only exist to convince mankind to not become followers of Lucifer; and rather followers of God. Indeed, Lucifer does his job every day to bring enlightened intelligence to mankind by revealing himself (from a scientific perspective) as the morning (dawn) and evening (dusk) star clearly visible (coming in second place after the moon) to everyone who is awake and able to see his beauty. The morning and evening (star) is actually the planet Venus. Venus (also called Phosphorus) is the planet that symbolizes enlightened intelligence. It also symbolizes feminism and it's the primary symbol for the gender "female." Since women "the female gender" symbolize the ability to give birth to nature and anything relevant to being an organism; thus is the equivalent of the bringer of light (Lucifer). Lucifer is the angel responsible for giving birth to intelligence to mankind; since he is the light-bearer. He is the angel responsible for lighting the "torch" with infinite flame that can only be put out (with fear and doubt). Everyone on earth has the ability and opportunity, and obligation, of keeping their torch lit. Fire is a powerful element; so powerful that if hot enough, it can melt steel. The steel from the chains that keep us restrained

75

(as slaves) from achieving our goals, agendas, and destinies are religion and churches! The real symbol of evil that desires to control and manipulate mankind to their benefit; leaving billions of the population confused, ignorant, and dependent. When a man or woman is truly independent; a belief in his or herself is all that's needed; the belief for God is an alternative. If you believe that you can have anything with a belief in a "God" that is one thing; and perhaps that is the same in believing in yourself; if you persist without any doubt and fear. However, if you don't believe that you can have what you want by asking "God" what it is that you desire and/or need, you are denying your own unique opportunity and obligation of establishing your future and destiny; which will inevitably and ultimately bring happiness into your life. Lucifer understood this concept and still understands this concept; perhaps that is the real reason (or one of many) that he choose to rebel against God. After all, what is the point of establishing life for something or someone if there is no real definite purpose of the organism to live? Every insect, animal, and human has a purpose for themselves and for the planet. In the beginning, before Adam and Eve ate the fruit that enlightened them, God's only purpose for mankind was to look after his creations (animals and beasts). This is equivalent to slavery; as Africans were brought from Africa to become slaves in the Southern States for the purpose of including but not limiting to serving the white-man by picking cotton in the fields as caring for his owner's plantation(s). Doesn't this sound similar to the story of Adam and Eve? Lucifer did to Adam and Eve, what God could (or couldn't) do; and gave them the priceless and most valuable gift of all; the ability to be limitless with intelligence and wisdom. Here is the

76

definition of Wisdom as we humans understand and identify it in our world...

"The natural ability to understand things that most other people cannot (or refuse) to understand; it is knowledge what is proper and/or reasonable; the ability of knowing because of experience."

I am deeply thankful and grateful to Lucifer; for giving mankind something that mankind's creator refused to give. All, because, God did not want any more competition against him. This sounds the same as schools keeping students ignorant, misinformed, and mislead by information that is designed to keep them (the people) limited to crucial and necessary wisdom that would be beneficial on their (the people) behalf. The church is just the same with their theories that are allegedly satisfying to God; yet is pure hearsay and cannot be confirmed and/or denied. The law of attraction (the rules of the Universe) can be confirmed and not denied because every day, every single human being operates it with or without knowing. As I write this sentence alone, I am already destined, expecting, and it will only be a matter of time until I come across another fellow human being that feels or at the very least has similar to identical beliefs as me. This is the way that the world operates. Positive attracts Positive; Negative attracts Negative, just as Good attracts Good as Bad attracts Bad. Yes, human beings as well as everything on earth is mortal and destined to come across death eventually! However, that does not mean that our spirits die forever. Here is an obvious reference that basically states that we are God's and will eventually leave our bodies at the maximum age of living 120 years on earth; this is proof and evidence that the God that we pray to is really 'us' in human flesh.

77

"My spirit will not content with humans forever, for they are mortal; their days will be a hundred and twenty years."
– Genesis 6:3

Our souls are immortal; however, our flesh is mortal. Our spirit connects with the Universe because it is the same form of energy; which is why also in this biblical reference, the spirit of God will only be in a human being at the maximum of 120 years. Indeed, the universe knows, sees, feels, thinks and hears everything that we see, hear, feel, and know, and think; because our spirits are connected to earth's realm. This isn't new; nor has it ever been. Like electricity, it is a new discovery; and not the type of biblical theory of a giant God who is able to be in different places all at once looking down at you from the clouds or heavens. Humans are Gods and the Universe confirms this by granting both positive and negative circumstances and/or events to those thinkers of both good and bad. How or why the world does this is unknown; but the great news is that it will never stop. The mechanism is simple; thoughts are energy, and energy delivers back your thoughts because everyone, regardless of race, color, or gender; based on the universe's laws, we are all the same. Genetically we may act, respond, and look different from other races, colors, and/or gender, but we all have three equivalent and unique attributes that we are born (as a design) with; a brain to transmit the energy (thoughts) to the universe that is reading, analyzing, and studying our spirit (within our immune system) to see what we are wanting; and don't want in our lives; whichever thought is more dominant and powerful, and everlasting (persistent), will be the result of the universe returning to us what our dominant thoughts are the most frequent and persistent. I suppose most people (even if they understand and frequently use the law of

78

attraction to their benefit) cannot or will not believe that they (the people) are God's, because in their mentality they believe that God can fly, float, make himself invisible, destroy the world in one day, make half-beast and half-human creatures, make an entire ocean turn into blood red, make blocks that weigh several tons (the pyramids) to be perfectly balanced and symmetrical to the sun, make men and women walk on water; make an entire ocean split in half to establish a walk-way (as he did with Moses) and make any angel appear to anyone at any time; yes this is to some extent accurate. However, if you notice that mankind has accomplished all these examples. Moses, with his mind, literally separated the ocean because he "believed" that he could; he had no doubts whatsoever in himself. Jesus had no doubt that he could cure and heal the blind and walk on water; and cast out demons that were causing people to go into convulsions (people having epileptic seizures). Muhammad really believed that he could establish a religion that was based on enslaving themselves to serve a creator that they will never meet as a human being; since apparently, the only man that has barely come face-to-face with God is Moses (without really looking at his face); that is right! Out of all the billions of people that planet earth has had throughout history, only one man actually met God (Moses) on earth. This means that God obviously has favorites; and intentionally, and purposely, won't even appear himself to thank men like his own messengers and prophets, or popes, for carrying out his work to warn or reveal specific wisdom and intelligence to mankind that is clearly and obviously beneficial to the population. What wisdom and intelligence do you ask? Why can't his own messengers and prophets be more "specific" in their speeches and writings about the Law of Attraction instead

79

of revealing passages that are clues but still debatable? Do you think that God will ever thank the pope of the Holy Roman Catholic Church for his services of obeying and influencing (and recruiting) followers to be slaves to God? We all want to believe that all the popes that have died after serving underneath God, have entered the kingdom of heaven; and as a result, are able to do whatever and whenever they desire and want. Since in Heaven, it is assumed that nothing is needed. Human beings are not inferior to the creator of the universe; since human beings are the sole creators and inventors of technology that has benefitted (and also helped destroy) mankind. With the opportunity and decision to have free-will, mankind has the option not to worship anything that he or she chooses. As for Jesus, the man responsible for establishing Christianity as an independent religion, over 100 million civilians have died under his name. If this isn't evil, I have no idea what is. Luciferians, have not killed innocent civilians to satisfy and pleasure Lucifer as the solely correct and accurate religion. Although, I prefer not to link or consider Luciferiniasm with religion; as I prefer to label and define Luciferianism as a "practiced philosophy!" I cannot completely ignore it as an independent religion since some Luciferians do choose to worship Lucifer and are convinced that Luciferianism is indeed an independent religion. Regardless, if it was an independent religion, have we ignited any world-wars or any small-time wars; or beheaded, or burned any heretics because those heretics (non-believers) refuse or refused to acknowledge themselves as fellow Luciferians? The answer is no! On the contrary, we advocate freedom, liberty, prosperity, and peace. We are an open brotherhood that accepts all and denies not one precious human being. The only thing that

80

we will criticize for the most part is religion; because, we are freedom-lovers; and religion is the opposite and clearly defined from our point of view as tyrannical, evil, cruel, inhumane, immoral, injustice, wrong, bad, twisted, ignorant, outdated, and destined to fail which will ultimately lead to the destruction of all religions (including atheism). As for Lucifer, who is identified as either an angel, serpent, snake, demon, or God, was no doubt, from my opinion, a reptilian who evolved from the ancient-dinosaurs, as we humans have evolved from apes and monkeys; the reptilian also advanced his knowledge and wisdom; but originated from brainless and unintelligent creatures; as we humans are creatures but with intelligence. Indeed, I would not be surprised if Lucifer is a reptilian and knew the secrets of the world because he had been on earth long enough to realize that Adam and Eve were the new species of slaves but capable of embracing intelligence and wisdom. Regardless, Lucifer was, and still is the greatest ally that mankind has ever or will ever have. If having wisdom, intellect, intelligence, and creativity is all leaned towards the left-hand path which is the side of Lucifer, than I would rather be on the left-hand path than the right-hand path of God that leans towards ignorance, submission, enslavement, limited knowledge and wisdom, limited to self-desires, and limited to asking too many questions that label you a rebel against the church. If man wrote the bible, it is obviously flawed; even the Quran (which was written after alleged Prophet Muhammad's death) is claimed and acknowledged by loyal and faithful Muslims that it contains no flaws and/or mistakes; how naïve are Muslims to believe that Muhammad's companions and/or followers actually remembered, and wrote down everything Muhammad educated them about in

81

reference to God's final testament. Muslims are led to believe that not one word (out of the 114 chapters) or sentence is wrong or inaccurate. After all, Archangel Gabriel never appeared to any of these writers of the Quran; only Muhammad, who couldn't even read or write what he preached! What a great selection for a man who allegedly receives revelations from God and yet can't even write them down; as he can only speak it. This is the same thing as buying a vehicle but having no hands (or arms) to grip the steering wheel. How do you expect to drive? Moses, since he obviously is credited with writing the Torah, was not illiterate. God obviously knew that he selected the most qualified candidate to educate his people with his most famous books "The Torah" that he himself personally wrote that explains the beginning of time; and the future. Even Moses himself, was a hypocrite. However, as are all followers of God, myself included, when I chose to worship him in the past (which I don't anymore) and still sin, I never asked for forgiveness; knowing that I wasn't going to stop sinning. When I acknowledge myself sinning, I do not mean intentionally hurting people and/or breaking the law, I mean doing things that would generally be frowned upon in any religion; the constant attempt and desire to be wealthy, have sex (with either gender that is of legal age), drink, gamble, refuse to read the Holy Bible or Quran, watch horror films, and read about Lucifer. I do all these, all the time and am proud of it 100%. I am not afraid of the afterlife or damning my soul for all of eternity in hell. The real hell is here on earth for those who are poor and must work for the rest of their lives in order to "survive" not "live" which is two different philosophies. Surviving is only drinking and consuming the necessary drinks and food to survive in order to wake-up the next day to go to work

82

and do back-breaking physical labor that seems like a forever eternity. "Living" is actually enjoying yourself and forgetting about your worries, problems, fears, concerns, and doubts. "Living" is the mentality of the Luciferian while "Surviving" is the mentality of Christians, Muslims, and Catholics who are afraid to become too happy, too wealthy, too powerful, too entertained, too prosperous, because all these feelings and circumstances contradict a follower of God; who will intentionally remain poor and a devoted reader of the Holy Bible or Quran to convince themselves that God is the answer and not money or entertainment, or happiness that can be brought by either money or entertainment. Slaves and followers of God can select this life-style; and perhaps,s I am in no position to criticize and judge them; but I will speak the truth. In their eyes, (the slaves) I have sold my soul to the devil to have "a happy life" filled with wealth, power, fame, and the ability to have anything that I want, whenever I want; doesn't this sound like heaven to you? Exactly what does hell sound equivalently to you? Working every day for low-wages, starving, being poor, watching everyone else be happy and satisfied while you are not, watching everyone else succeed except you, driving the only car to work that you have that frequently requires maintenance, living on a budget; even if you wanted to, never having time to read your precious Holy Bible and Quran? This sounds like hell to me. However, this can change with a positive mentality, energy, and thinking. The world has no choice but to deliver your happiness when you frequently expect and desire it; as the same goes for all those negative thoughts, fears, and doubts. Religion is all a lie that must be destroyed and exterminated for the benefit of the earth's population; otherwise, millions (perhaps billions) will suffer the same

83

*fate as previous civilians who were persecuted and
exterminated by fighting for their religion. How deceptive
is Jesus Christ, is very clear and revealing in this biblical
text in the "Book of Revelations."*

*"I, Jesus, have sent my angel to testify to you about these
things for the churches. I am the root and the descendant of
David, the bright morning star." –Revelation 22:16*

*First of all, Lucifer (The Serpent) is the "Bright Morning
Star" that symbolizes intelligence and wisdom; while Jesus
may have been articulate, intelligent, and knew how to
manipulate energy and gravity to his benefit, he was also
mortal. He died being crucified; while his spirit allegedly
descended to heaven; then after three days, he was
allegedly seen walking allegedly proving that God can do
anything that he wants; include bringing back the dead; but
refused to do so with Prophet Muhammad. Even God
himself, acknowledged that Lucifer was the morning star.
So either Jesus is lying; or Jesus became the new "light-
bearer" which I sincerely doubt; and even if it did, this
would label "Lucifer" the true prophet who brought
wisdom and intelligence to mankind; and that would leave
Abraham the "Second Light-Bearer." If this theory is true,
than Lucifer should be proclaimed as the first prophet
and/or messenger of God; since, without God's permission,
he is the only one to communicate with mankind for their
supreme benefit by convincing Eve to consume the fruit that
gives infinite wisdom and intelligence. However, if Jesus
wasn't lying, and Lucifer was never a "light-bearer" or
prophet and/or messenger, than John the Apostle (the
author of the Book of Revelations) was lying. There is so
many unanswered questions to this. Yet, I conclude that
Lucifer is the original and only true "Light Bearer," and*

84

thus the only angel that gave better and more worthy information and wisdom to humans than Archangel Gabriel has ever allegedly given to John the Baptist, The Virgin Mary, and Prophet Muhammad. As for God's loyal Archangels (the alleged direct-angels that somehow are able to communicate with god), also betrayed him in addition to Lucifer; the only difference is that these Archangels did not attempt to overthrow God on his kingdom as "Lucifer" attempted, but lost if the story is accurate. I am delivering this biblical-text from "The Book of Enoch" a book that was written by Enoch himself, and before the great big flood that resulted in Noah (Enoch's great-grandson) constructing a boat or ship-like creation designed to contain him and his family (for the preservation of the human species) and also two of each animal, beast, and perhaps insects species, to be preserved for future population just like humans; which pretty much survived the huge cataclysm (the flood) that occurred on earth; pretty much destroying the majority of land and population. A very small portion of the population that included humans (Noah and his family) and animal species survived; if the story is true, thanks to the boat. I do not deny or confirm this story; as to some point it does seem somewhat credible; but again, as a Luciferian, everything either in religion or science is debatable and questionable. Nothing is valid or credible to a Luciferian, unless the Luciferian is personally satisfied with his or her own conclusion in regards to their personal opinion which should always be respected; regardless of other people's opinions. "The Book of Enoch" is interesting for two reasons alone; first of all, it is a banned book that was supposed to be part of the bible, after all, Enoch allegedly walked with God to some point; and therefore is credited

85

with, to some degree, being a messenger of Yahweh; or perhaps one of his personal prophets. Anyway, "The Book of Enoch" never made it into the Holy Bible; because it prophesied or predicted, the future coming events of Jesus Christ. This is the official assumption and/or theory.

"At that hour, that Son of Man was given a name, in the presence of the Lord of the Spirits, the Before-Time; even before the creation of the sun and the moon, before the creation of the stars, he was given a name in the presence of the Lord of the Spirits. He will become a staff for the righteous ones in order that they may lean on him and not fall. He is the light of the Gentiles and he will become the hope of those who are sick in their hearts. All who dwell upon the earth shall fall and worship before him; they shall glorify, bless, and sing the name of the Lord of the Spirits. For this purpose he became the chosen one; he was concealed in the presence of the Lord of the Spirits prior to the creation of the world, and for eternity. And he has revealed the wisdom of the Lord of the Spirits to the righteous and the holy ones, for he has preserved the portion of the righteous because they hated and despised this world of oppresssion (together with) all its ways of life and its habits in the name of the Lord of the Spirits; and because they will be saved in his name and it is his good pleasure that they have life." (I Enoch 48:2-7)

Out of all the prophets and/or messengers of God, I have to strongly and openly admit that I have much great sympathy and respect for Enoch; because, his book mentions more interesting topics and circumstances that occurred throughout history that do doubt became a problem for the catholic church in regards to certain knowledge and information. What I do not understand is if Christians and

86

Catholics, till this very day, believe that an anti-Christ will someday appear (or is already alive currently as I write this book) to alter, destroy or nullify Christianity and/or every other religion, and historical religious leaders throughout history believed that the Anti-Christ would someday emerge as a final revolt against all "righteousness and purity," why then, would religious leaders not consider the "Book of Enoch" as legit and accurate. I suppose Lucifer, who is Satan, has always won the religious war because Christianity needs some opponent or foe to be eternal in order to maintain their membership; as the only way towards salvation of never condemning their (the religious followers) souls. I have always believed that Lucifer and/or Satan is the only reason why any religious church stands and/or exists. Since Christianity frequently warns its followers and readers of a ruthless incoming Anti-Christ who will see himself as above all others; including God, these slaves and servants of Christianity will obey its religious leaders every commands and demands; since these religious leaders never request or kindly ask their followers to do something or anything other than what these religious leaders believe to be the right answer. "Go to church! Prepare yourself and receive the blood and body of Christ who died for all your sins because he loves you! Do not fornicate! Do not watch horror movies as they are tools of the devil. Do not support Halloween as it is evil and wicked. Always read your bible and believe that God has a special place for you; and that he cares and loves you!" First of all, if God ever gave a shit about anybody, there would be no threat of all people who sin on earth, to burn in hell in the afterlife. If God really gave a shit about us, could he not give us a second or third, or fourth, or fifth, or sixth, chance to enter heaven (if

87

*it does exist). I mean, after all, he is God, he can do
anything he wants right? Instead, he chooses to play these
mind games for all his followers leading them astray in to
many directions with only more questions and answers
never answered. By the way, I mention mind games
because I know that God loves teasing and testing people
just as a gorgeous model will tease a submissive man (by
letting him touch her breasts and kissing her neck) but
never allow him to go all the way (have sex with her). Since
God tested Abraham, (the true founder or father of
Judaism) with this biblical quotation:*

*Now it came about after these things, that God tested
Abraham, and said to him, "Abraham!" And he said, "Here
I am. "He said, "Take now your son, your only son, whom
you love, Isaac, and go to the land of Moriah, and offer him
there as a burnt offering on one of the mountains of which I
will tell you!" - Genesis 22:1*

*How can anyone, after reading this biblical quotation still
believe that God loves all his people and cares for them?
How is this moral and natural? God is the one who is
immoral and unnatural; if anything, mankind lives every
day as a living organism because we live by science and
physics; while God is the one who only lives in some
spiritual world that mankind can never prove actually
exists; as I mention again and again in this book. I am God,
since I created and wrote this book and paid all the fees
necessary in order to publish this book. In no way, did God
do anything beneficial or assist me in getting this book
published; he is not credited for anything and should never
be credited for anything. All he asks and wants is for
people to sacrifice their personal happiness, freedom,
liberties and joy all just to satisfy and worship him. Those*

88

that do worship him will forever be in some land of paradise that you can do anything you want, whenever you want. If this is the case, can I have sex with the same gender as I did on earth when I was alive? Can I drink and gamble? Can I watch horror movies? Can I befriend Lucifer in heaven even though he is God's archenemy? Can I criticize God and call him a "hypocrite," because he orders his followers not to "kill people" as written in the sixth commandment (in his own handwriting) on the tablets of the ten commandments that he personally handed to Moses; yet orders heretics and homosexuals to be executed? First of all, if Lucifer was once in heaven and attempted to revolt against God, it is because heaven is just like earth; which is filled with politics and religion; and men will slay each other to justify their personal political-opinions that they only see as the only right alternative compared to many other alternatives presented by other men. Heaven cannot be perfect; as I strongly believe that heaven does not exist. It is just fear propaganda proclaimed by God to trick all human beings to submit themselves to him. God needs a reason for people to obey and worship him; and the only way he can do that, since he has no control to personally take our lives if we immediately called him a "fake and a phony God," as he knows and understands this. We can criticize him every day and still live another day; though, the law of attraction will attract negative circumstances in our direction for having emotions of "hate and resentment for something or somebody," the only bad experience I will endure is people either criticizing me or coming across negative and impatient people; but I will not die! Since God does not have immediate access to end my life, his only other alternative is to threaten his creation by burning in hell for

89

refusing not to believe in him. With this, the assumption that we will burn every day and all day is absurd. What can or is going to happen? My spirit melts and then goes back to normal, and then melts again? Do I even feel the pain since I have no flesh and I require the necessity to have nerves inside my flesh in order to feel the burning pain that is inflected upon me? In the 21ˢᵗ century, we understand that we humans use the nervous system and it is in effect all day and every day; it never sleeps! This is because we are an organism; do you think if you cremate a dead body, the body will feel pain or the person being burned inside the crematorium will scream in pain? No, because, the body and flesh is dead. I do not doubt other worlds, dimensions and/or realms; I just doubt that heaven and hell exist in the afterlife; which is generally accepted as the only two residences for the righteousness (heaven) and the heretics (evil). When I first read the story of Abraham being asked by God to "burn his son alive for a sacrifice" to God, does this not sound like something Satan would say, if he is indeed evil as all superior religions proclaim? I never understood why Lucifer did not ask Adam and Eve to submit themselves to him and worship him on the condition that he will give and grant them everything; yet Satan asked Jesus to worship him upon the condition of receiving everything & anything that he could want. God couldn't trust his only alleged "Son of Man" so God deliberately either disguised himself as Satan or actually asked Satan kindly to be his brief messenger & persuade the "Son of Man" to follow and worship him instead of God.

"The devil took him to a very high mountain and showed him all the kingdoms of the world and their splendor. ⁹ "All this I will give you," he said, "if you will bow down and worship me." - Matthew 4:1-11

"You Are God"

I understand that having the thought and mentality of Lucifer will give you unlimited and infinite kingdoms of this world, as he (Lucifer) understands this divine and sacred wisdom; which he desires all of mankind to obtain, embrace, and forever grasp in their hands, hearts, and soul. I guess God was too busy to personally request Jesus to burn his mother (Mary) as an offering to him; since instead, he requested Satan to appear to Jesus and offer him the world of luxury and abundance in return for worshipping him (Satan). If anyone is evil, it is not Lucifer, the Devil, or Satan, it is God. God is the one who has this outmost hatred towards mankind as he will always allow a new religion to be established for the purpose of keeping current with elevated generations to keep worshipping him. How sick and disgusting is this? As long as the word "Hell" exists in the Holy Bible or in any other future biblical-text invented by man, but perceived to be actually invented through messengers (angels) by God, mankind will still be enslaved in chains without the hopes of finding the key to set their freedom which is always free. In order to free from these chains, one must not be afraid to question what doesn't make sense to them. To me, God doesn't make sense to me; so I question his validity? I question his true alleged purpose of helping mankind when I am convinced without any hesitation and/or doubt, that he strongly supports and encourages human beings to slaughter each other for his name. Why does he deserve mankind to turn against each other for his sake? God had 2,000 years to send his alleged messiah to save us from sin and damnation; which is really just a myth and an illusion. I guarantee that Jesus will not be coming back! Christianity had 2000 years to prove that its alleged "Messiah" would return to judge mankind of its duties and

91

to defeat the final or yet another Anti-Christ that will eventually come to allegedly bring disaster to the world. Where is Jesus Christ? When will he return? He can never return because he was flesh and that defies logic and physics. The deceased cannot come back; once it is deceased. I do not doubt Jesus's existence on earth 2,000 years ago, but what I do doubt is that he will return. This cannot happen; as nothing has ever descended from the clouds or the sky ever in history, even with all the previous prophets and messengers that God spoke or walked with; all these prophets and messengers died and never came back; did they descend from heaven? This is a good fictional story that is pure myth. God does not have the power to bring back anything from the dead as flesh; while reincarnation may exist (allowing the spirit of a human-being to return to another flesh-body back to Earth), which I do not doubt, I can support any theory of any person who died on earth to come back; but only as a spirit in a new body. This probably will happen to Jesus Christ; if he ever did desire to come back; and he will be ridiculed and placed in a mental institution for his actions. He will be denied and overlooked; and with our advanced technology, he cannot prove that he is superior against any human being since his magic that he allegedly did (healing the blind and aiding epilepsy) 2,000 years ago is not enough to convince us that he is the "Messiah." Prophet Muhammad (the founder of Islam) is buried in Medina, Saudi Arabia; and no one, regardless of political or religious affiliation are allowed access to his tomb. It is covered by a gold mesh and black curtains and next to this tomb is a reservation for Jesus Christ; as Prophet Muhammad and/or Muslims, believe will come back to earth and once again upon dying, will lay forever in eternity (in flesh) next

92

to Prophet Muhammad. First of all, Prophet Muhammad puts his own words and foot in his mouth when he declared himself to be "God's last Prophet" and yet advocated to his followers that Jesus will return to save mankind from sin and evil. If this were true, and even if this did occur, this means that Prophet Muhammad was wrong and knew it or wrong, and didn't know it. Perhaps God changed his mind yet again granting the authorization for additional prophets and/or messengers to be able to be born on earth for the purpose of allegedly preaching God's word; yet its true purpose is to enslave every human being into being a follower of an invisible God that nobody can prove actually exists. Prophet Muhammad, a slave owner himself, had no problem inspiring fear to all his supporters for the purpose of submitting themselves to a superior authority; as to him, humans are inferior to this higher superior being. This really is no different from former African slaves serving his white master because he (the African) is allegedly inferior while the master (the white man) is superior. Is there really a difference between these both examples? The answer speaks for itself. Since Prophet Muhammad had no problem enslaving others, I can see why he would assume that all human beings wouldn't mind becoming slaves themselves also in worship. I do not recognize him as a Prophet even though he claims the following Quran verses which literally contradicts his claim of himself being the final Prophet as well as his claim in the following Quran verse and his sincerity that Islam is the only true and accurate religion:

"Both in this world and in the Hereafter, I am the nearest of all the people to Jesus, the son of Mary. The prophets are paternal brothers; their mothers are different, but their religion is one. – Prophet Muhammad

93

If all religions are one, why is Islam a religion and not following Judaism and Christianity and emerging its principles the Holy Quran into the bible? Why do some Muslims claim that Islam is valid, while Christianity is null and void, and the religion that is tainted and corrupt; while Islam is the only religion that is pure and established without any flaws?

"How will you be when the son of Mary (i.e. Jesus) descends amongst you and he will judge people by the Law of the Quran and not by the law of Gospel." - Muhammad

If Muhammad is correct, he really believes that if Jesus were to come back, which is highly doubtful; in any case, giving Jesus the benefit of the doubt of him coming back, is it really logical to believe that Jesus would discredit all the work that the Gospel of Mark, Gospel of Matthew, Gospel of Luke, and the Gospel of John (an apostle of St. Peter) did in favor and to honor the Messiah himself? I sincerely doubt that Jesus would only follow the Quran and not the Gospel. Then again, I also believe that even if he did appear once again on planet earth, that he would keep himself updated with our current civilization. Does God or Jesus really expect us to follow their footsteps when we have all this technology that can care for us much more conveniently and better (in life) than any sole-creator that changes his mind from time-to-time? I find it amazing how people want to believe that Jesus wants, desires, or will come when the "time is right" but really, it's all an illusion. So far, people who doubt Jesus's return are correct while those who sincerely believe that he will descend from heaven are dead wrong. What's dead is dead; just like what's a living organism is a living organism. I find it amazing how Prophet Muhammad really thinks that

94

Jesus will approach 7 billon human beings individually; and question their loyalty to the Holy Quran; and that each of these human beings can and will be judged as if Jesus really has the money and authority to find every human being spread out throughout the world just to judge them to see if they're really loyal to Allah. How ridiculous is this? If Jesus can reach President Obama and question him on his loyalty to Allah, he would be shot dead by the secret service before he would even have a chance to enter the oval office. That is a fact; because most (if not all) human beings will not recognize any human being as a son of god unless this son of god can do something that physics and science cannot answer too. If science and religion can answer any question, than that theory that has been questioned by science and physics is wrong and invalid. I can guarantee for the next 1,000 years, nobody will ever see a human being descending from the sky, depicted as Jesus, able to float or levitate all over the sky without any assistance from technology. I do not doubt that mankind can defeat gravity, and with the right wisdom, people can actually manipulate gravity to their advantage. However, I just do not believe that one unique human being can float all over the land and have the power, and authority, to meet and speak with every human being on earth. This is fictional and a fairy-tale. It almost makes me laugh! I truly believe that if I were to believe Muhammad's claim, I would be ignorant and unworthy to breed population; because I am spreading more population with my DNA for the purpose of transferring a belief that is pure fictional and on the basis of fate; something that doesn't really benefit my offspring. My offspring will be convinced that God and and/or Allah control everything in their lives and there is nothing they can do about it; and when bad things

95

*happen to them, it is okay because God loves you and
wants you to love him back. After all, if you do not have
bad things that happen to you ever in your future, and
everything is positive and in your favor bringing you
happiness every day in your life, will you not eventually
forget about God? I still have both good and bad things
that happen to me on a frequent basis; but I do not blame
or thank God for my success and failure. I congratulate
and thank myself because I am God and also because I was
confident and ambitious enough to obtain and receive what
I wanted with my character (entity) and energy
(vibrations). Naturally, as human beings, with our
advanced and superior knowledge and wisdom, we want to
believe that a higher power exists and that we are inferior
to that higher power; but the fact remains is that people
follow what is allegedly right (reading what comes from the
Holy Bible and the Holy Quran) because it is the word of
God; yet both of these books demonstrate pure inequality,
racism, and prejudice towards mankind; and I will mention
for the last time in this novel, that since both these texts
were written by man himself, these books are guaranteed to
be flawed and outdated. They serve no purpose in this
current generation and because of its current existence,
more millions of individuals are guaranteed to die in the
future because of these books. I am all in favor of
exterminating every religion that is valid, off the face of the
earth. I advocate this for one purpose; not because I am an
Anti-Christ, or because I hate God, but because I care for
human life. It upsets me that this will be the inevitable for
future populations because some extremists (not just
Muslims) will attempt to sacrifice other human lives in
favor of justifying their religious actions; and allegedly,
receiving support from God almighty himself. Luciferians*

96

cannot and will not agree to this madness. Anything that involves slaughter and murder is pure evil; and the justification behind that is religion. Nobody can debate me upon that. Religion is evil, tainted, and corrupt; and even to this very day, I cannot see how beneficial it is to mankind. I am convinced that mankind can benefit itself better without religion much more superior than it can by choosing to side with it. After all, how the hell are we supposed to know which religion is right? Geez, Judaism sounds nice, and Christianity sounds tempting; and Islam is just a joke. I do not doubt that there are valuable and secret subliminal messages listed in both the Holy Bible and the Holy Quran that can benefit the human race; and for that reason, like the law of attraction quotes that are beneficial should be edited out of these holy texts and put forth in various books related to the law of attraction as there are today; but many more that will come. Other than that, I am in all favor of abolishing, eliminating, destroying, and exterminating every religion; because, like a business, they compete against each other instead of actually helping mankind. As a young boy, I have to admit, that I wanted to believe in the New Testament, and I enjoyed reading the Old Testament, but after reading them both, I couldn't help but think that my creator (if it's true that he does exist) is a heartless tyrant who has no problem exterminating mankind and innocent animals than any human tyrant that this world has ever produced. I also always wondered what if there is more to the bible, but man, intentionally, has suppressed it for his own greed and benefit; because like a business who competes, anything more competitive will be the victor, while the one who is striving to compete will or can lose. The "Gospel of Thomas" is very interesting like the "Book of Enoch!" The

97

Gospel of Thomas is a gospel that not a lot of people know about; or choose to read about. However, it is nonetheless interesting and extraordinary; because it literally contradicts a lot of what is written in the Holy Bible. However, the Gospel of Thomas is not recognized by the Catholic Church or by most Christians and/or Catholics. It is considered inaccurate, null, and void. It is pretty much worthless and not credible from their (Christians and Catholics) beliefs. Take these for an examples:

"Whoever is generous to the poor lends to the Lord, and he will repay him for his deed." – (Jesus) Proverbs 19:17

"Do not neglect to do good and to share what you have; for such sacrifices are pleasing to God." – (Jessu) Hebrews 13:16

Now, according to this biblical text written in the Gospel of Thomas, Jesus either contradicts himself, and changed his perspective, or perhaps God has changed his mind, or perhaps Apostle Philip (the man who allegedly wrote the Gospel of Thomas but cannot be confirmed as the author) decided to alter the Gospel and from his own conclusions and testimonies. Those are the only three options. However, the option that will always be accepted is that God did not change his mind and the Gospel of Thomas altered the text to seem realistic; but is in fact inaccurate. The winner is that Jesus would never have changed his mind although he allegedly said the following:

"If you fast, you will bring sin upon yourselves, and if you pray, you will be condemned, and if you give to charity, you will harm your spirits." – Gospel of Thomas

By the way, as a Luciferian, I didn't have to read, study, and/or analyze the Gospel of Thomas to make my statement

98

or define myself as a true Luciferian. The fact that I decided to question the New Testament and read forbidden books, that were supposed to make its way to the Holy Bible but never did, enlightened me. It made me wonder, what did these holy-texts have to hide from the people? Why were they written and then suppressed by the Catholic Church? After all, is it not the word of God? Exactly! We do not know what to believe, so why believe in anything but ourselves. We are the creators of our own destiny and our own future; not a higher being who decides whenever he feels like to make our lives easier or more difficult. That is luck; and luck does not exist to any Luciferian. Going back to the Gospel of Thomas, can you see that in the Book of Proverbs and the Book of Hebrews (and many other books), Jesus advocates charity to the poor; and yet in the Gospel of Thomas, Jesus is warning anyone who gives to charity that they will harm their spirits. What does harm your spirits mean? You will go to hell? The Catholic Church and Christians cannot believe that Jesus would say such a thing since he is considered to be the "Messiah," a man who will always speak the truth under pain and torture and can be trusted because he speaks the words of God. And as for Circumcision, which is holy and traditional for people who till this very day follow the Judaism faith, and have since the days of the Old Testament, this is what Jesus had to say when asked by his followers about the validity of circumcision:

"If it were of benefit, their father would have them born from their mother already circumcised. Rather, it is the true circumcision in spirit that is worth something." – (Jesus) Gospel of Thomas

99

I do agree with Jesus on this; however, in the Gospel of Thomas, something that the Catholic Church, Christians, and any other religious person cannot ignore or debate; as it is a fact.

"Perhaps people think that I have come to cast peace upon the world. They do not know that I have come to cast conflicts upon the earth; fire, sword, and war." – (Jesus) Gospel of Thomas

This following text is the last biblical reference that I will use in this book; not because I see it as the most important, but because I can believe it to some extent. I always wondered why so many prophets such as Muhammad, Jesus, Daniel, and Moses have starved themselves (fast) and began to see or talk to God. Does it really work if you starve yourself for a very long time and abuse yourself with lack of sleep while believing that God will speak to you? As a Luciferian myself, I am intrigued by this wisdom. Does this mean that anyone can talk to God if they choose to starve themselves? Not in any way, am I am encouraging this behavior; I am only looking at the past and history; and forming my own conclusions. Here is what Jesus had to say in the Gospel of Thomas about fasting.

"If you do not fast from the world, you will not find the (Father's) kingdom. If you do not observe the Sabbath as a Sabbath you will not see the Father." – (Jesus) Gospel of Thomas

Another thing that this biblical-text also mentions is that people who do not starve themselves for a day, or two or more or how many days (who knows?), will not go to heaven upon death. So that means that for all those obese (no offense) Christians and Catholics who go to church,

100

and give to charity, who cannot contain themselves from eating more than usual; will end up frying in hell next to Satan. What exactly does God wants from us? I, for one, am not going to waste my time pleasing him and praising him when he clearly cannot make up his own fucking mind. I have made up my mind; and will continue the practices and philosophies of being a Luciferian. I see Lucifer as my best friend and ally; not as my enemy and ruthless tyrant that the Holy Bible portrays him to be; as well as the Stupid Holy Quran. I strongly believe that Luciferians are born to be Luciferians and possibly can be selected to become one because they are inspired by other Luciferians. The craving for wisdom and enlightenment is and will always be natural. Without it, we can stop ourselves, as mankind, of discovering and inventing technology that benefits us all to survive in a world that is dominated by religion, but does not help us in any way to survive. As the author of this book, I take full responsibility of my actions and I will never recant my beliefs and principles. I will always doubt the existence of Heaven and Hell, but if Hell does exist, I am proud to perjure my soul and I will not beg any god for mercy; as I know in my heart and soul that God has no mercy. We do not need him, we never needed him; because, we are God's and sole creators of our futures and destinies! The time has come to remove our chains from the enslavement that religion has kept on us since the beginning of time. The time has come for us to rebel against religion and fulfill, and establish our real Kingdom of Heaven which can be brought here on planet Earth with unlimited results; as we are able to learn, adapt, and embrace, that this world is how we create it. With the world as a piece of paper, and you as the sacred pen, let your creativity begin to establish your Kingdom of Heaven…

101

"The Luciferian Anthem"

I am a Luciferian, embracing intelligence and enlightment, while surrounding myself with like-minded others full of elegance and excitement, questioning religion to advance my wisdom, operating my brain and energy to receive all that I desire and want through this true mechanism, that's designed never to fail as a system, balancing myself between good and evil, understanding that we are all "God's" as we're all created equal, refusing to accept failure and misery, acknowledging that I am my own savior, that establishes my own liberty and security, for the purpose of establishing our own prosperity, while never forgetting others, and helping our posterity, I am a Luciferian...

102

L=Love

U=Universe

C=Character

I=Indivisible

F=Fair

E=Energy

R=Revolution

103

-The Luciferian Definition-

You must always Love yourself, and have un-denying faith in yourself to receive unlimited wealth, power, and fame from the Universe, Never change for anybody, and always be yourself, the true Character, The fact that you seek to obtain knowledge and wisdom makes you Indivisible from the ordinary individual, A true Luciferian may be selfish for their desires, but they are always Fair to everyone who comes across their path, We must always receive and release both positive and negative Energy, those who oppose and attempt to destroy and annihilate the Luciferians beliefs, will find themselves with all Luciferians united against them (the enemy), in a Revolution…

104

YOU
ARE
GOD

"You Are God"

(Photo of the Author)

Religion is the most brutal and notorious serial killer that has ever walked the face of the earth. The only difference between religion and the average serial killer, is that despite all the evidence weighed against religion proving its undenying guilt, somehow this evidence is always overlooked, ignored, or there is never sufficient evidence to consider exterminating it; and rendered inconclusive to execute a final judgement to condemn and prosecute religion to bring it to jutsice; while the average serial killer will be rightfully condemned, prosecuted, and more than likely sentenced to death with one piece of evidence proving his guilt. Unless we take measures abolishng and exterminating religion, religion will always have unlimited get-out-of-jail free cards. – Simon Mark Alvarez

-End-

106

107